Annette is great at what she does, helping people own the room without losing themselves in it. *Step Into Your Spotlight* doesn't just teach confidence; it transforms how you show up when it matters most. Working with her taught me how to show up with more clarity, confidence and ease, on camera and off!
Nina Acosta, fractional executive

I absolutely recommend *Step Into Your Spotlight* to anyone ready to boost their confidence and self-belief. It's insightful, uplifting and full of down-to-earth guidance that truly makes change possible.
Sheila Granger, award-winning hypnotherapist, author and trainer

Annette is my first port of call when life gets tricky; her calm and reflective sense of self always allows the best ideas to flow to the surface. As a TV Exec myself who worked alongside Annette for more than twenty years at the BBC, I can say first-hand that she is the sounding board you need when times get tough and the challenges truly begin. I'm proud to call her a close friend and know that she is intuitively a kind and thoughtful person who brings out the best in those she meets. If you're in a corner, Annette will help you find your own way out!
Sid Cole FCGI, freelance TV executive and media consultant

She's the best Mum I've ever had!
Chelsea Williams, daughter

AF260554

What people have to say about *Step Into Your Spotlight* and Annette Williams

Read this book! Your favourite presenter has probably worked with Annette – and she's great!

Ortis Deley, TV presenter and actor

Before working with Annette, I'd presented at conferences and training days – but I always felt nervous and self-conscious. Annette's techniques completely transformed the way I approach being in the spotlight.

Since having sessions with her, I've gone on to deliver a keynote presentation and even appeared in a health documentary with confidence and ease. *Step Into Your Spotlight* captures the same insight, warmth, and practical guidance that helped me find my voice and truly enjoy being seen. This book is a game-changer for anyone who wants to feel calm, authentic and confident.

Dr Sue Peacock, consultant health psychologist

Annette saw something in me I didn't know I had, and I have her to thank for where I am today. If you want to be the best version of you, *Step Into Your Spotlight* is the book you need.

Angellica Bell, TV and radio presenter and author

I worked with Annette in Children's TV, an area I didn't know. She put me at my ease, helping enormously with any nerves I had. Her skills and experience shine through in *Step Into Your Spotlight* and I recommend it highly.

Les Dennis, actor and entertainer

Annette helps people make real, tangible progress towards their goals – especially when those goals involve confidence and self-belief. I know this first-hand because what we made together went out on air to over four million people and I knew I could trust her to support me, every step of the way.

Angela Lamont, Emcee and presenter

For twenty-seven years, Annette has been my mentor, giving me amazing advice. I have been able to pass this on to others, to help them realise their potential, like me. Read *Step Into Your Spotlight* and you'll be able to do the same!
Ewan Vinnicombe, editor #7 Blue Peter and project director: Freemantle, Channel 4

Everyone in TV needs someone they can be themselves with. We all have a 'work' version of ourselves, but with a trusted person alongside you, you can allow yourself to take down your 'work-shield' and be honest and vulnerable. Annette was – and still is – that person. Listen to what she has to say. You will be grateful and all the better for it.
Vanessa Amberleigh, Honorary Fellow, University of Winchester, award-winning TV executive and fitness guru

Step Into Your Spotlight is an empowering and insightful read. Annette brilliantly blends her TV expertise with her hypnotherapy practice to help readers unlock genuine self-belief and confidence. The book is full of practical and relatable techniques that truly work – it's like having Annette's calm, reassuring voice guiding you every step of the way. A must-read for anyone who wants to feel more confident.
Joanna Scott-Aspray, founder, The Cheshire Club

I love that Annette is essentially nicking all the tips and tricks from showbizland and giving them to you! Enjoy!
Lauren Layfield, TV and radio presenter and author

Annette has mentored me throughout my career, guiding me through numerous promotions, supporting me to take bold steps and helping me realise my potential. She is a wonderful, nurturing person who I still call on now.
Jennifer Morrison, series producer, The Great Pottery Throw Down

STEP INTO YOUR SPOTLIGHT

The TV insider's guide to feeling confident when all eyes are on YOU!

Written by
Annette Williams

This book is dedicated to my wonderful family and friends, but especially to Chelsea and Muffin.

Love You!

Foreword

Being in the limelight isn't always easy, and for many, it isn't even a preference.

There's that scenario of a pitch-black room, so dark you cannot see what is directly in front of you. The silence is so still that if a pin dropped, you would hear it loud and clear. Close your eyes and imagine being in that space. It is daunting. Then suddenly, there's a flick of a switch and a spotlight hits you. You are now visible, but you don't know to whom you are visible or what they are thinking. You are no longer in control.

I can relate to this. And I only have myself to blame because, to a certain extent, my career in broadcasting was my own doing. We make choices, and those choices come with consequences. I do, however, have to place some of the responsibility at the feet of **Annette Williams** – a successful children's television producer at the BBC twenty-five years ago. Yes, the Annette who has written this book!

Annette took the time to watch the showreel I had posted to her (along with a KitKat and a handwritten note!) and then contacted me to suggest a meeting to discuss possible presenting opportunities. I remember that day vividly, boarding a train to BBC Television Centre, unsure what to expect. We sat in a small office high enough to overlook West London, in the infamous East Tower where so many of the incredible children's BBC shows of the nineties and noughties were created. The meeting felt huge; it had the potential to change my life, which was overwhelming for someone at the start of their journey.

Annette asked why I wanted to be on television and whether I could handle the pressures of live broadcasting. I trusted her immediately. She knew her own mind and exactly what it took to create great television. Once she brought me on board, her expectations were clear. I often wonder what she saw in me that day that led to my first job in the industry. I had no idea if I could pull it off, but Annette believed in me, and I learned that for others to believe in us, we first must believe in ourselves.

When I think about the title of this book, *Step Into Your Spotlight*, and relate it to my own life, I realise I became even more aware of the spotlight when I auditioned to work on CBBC. This was the ultimate job. My audition, however, was terrible. Fear engulfed me and stole my ability to speak – not ideal when you're auditioning to be a presenter! Despite fluffing it, I was offered the contract, and overnight everything changed. Suddenly, I was presenting to millions of children every afternoon on BBC One, with no choice but to face my fears and find confidence fast. I threw myself into it, made mistakes along the way, but I kept going.

Most of us will, at some point in life, experience a moment like this. An unexpected opportunity appears; our inner critic creeps in and tries to deter us. It may not be television. It could be performing in a school play, a job interview, speaking in a meeting, or hosting a celebration for loved ones. Whatever it is when that spotlight hits us, we face a choice: do we step forward or do we step back?

That is why this book is such a valuable tool. It offers strategies to handle those moments and helps you find your voice and be authentically *you*. Confidence is layered, it cannot simply be labelled as something one person has and another doesn't. Many factors shape it and Annette unpacks these with warmth and wisdom. One thing I have learned is that confidence often arrives *after* we have gone through the challenge. Only once we have done the hard thing do we feel the reward, and that feeling is euphoric. It is empowering.

I know I could not have faced my fears without people who supported and encouraged me to be the best version of myself. You will know who those people are in your life, and if you haven't met them yet, don't worry, there is always time. Thankfully for me, Annette, who has since conquered yet another profession as a hypnotherapist (yes, she's annoyingly brilliant), remains a friend, and now, an author.

So, as you turn the pages of this empowering book, allow Annette to guide you towards a place where the spotlight feels less like exposure and more like home.

Angellica Bell

Contents:

Nothing gets the adrenaline pumping quite like the ten second countdown to: 'Live – On Air'!

How to Use This Book

Let me be clear...this is a book about boosting your confidence. It is not a guide to becoming a TV presenter. If that is your goal, I will happily point you towards brilliant colleagues who can help you with that.

But if you want to:

◊   Find your voice

◊   Speak up at work

◊   Deliver a compelling speech

◊   Apply for a promotion

◊   Say 'Yes' (or 'No') to something new

...then you are absolutely in the right place!

Please read this book with an open mind. Whoever you think you are right now is not set in stone. Confidence is a skill, and it can be learned. And I know that your future self will thank you for getting started.

What to expect

Each chapter contains a mix of practical exercises, personal stories, psychological insights and easy-to-use tools to help you assemble your own 'Confidence Toolbox'.

Some techniques are quick wins, which you can implement straight away. Others might require more reflection and practice. Both are equally helpful.

You might find it useful to keep a journal as you work your way through this book.

> *If you are anything like me, then you will love having a reason to go stationery shopping. 'Back to School' shopping was always a highlight at the end of my summer holidays!*

As you will be investing both your time and effort, why not treat yourself. Choose a beautiful notebook and use this to jot down your thoughts and make notes as you work your way through the exercises. Of course, you can jot down notes in this book, if you prefer. Personally, I don't like writing on books and prefer to keep mine separate, but you do you!

Writing things down can help you to process your thoughts, track your progress and reflect more deeply on what is changing for you. Journalling is a great way to stop thoughts from swirling around inside your head.

"It's better out than in!"

Shrek

Q: Anything else different about this book?

Yes, there are a few things which set this book apart:

- ◊ **The TV perspective:** You will be looking at confidence through the lens of the television industry, drawing on the tools and techniques I have learned from nearly four decades of working behind the scenes, alongside presenters, performers and production teams.

- ◊ **TV-inspired structure:** Like most live TV broadcasts, this book begins with a countdown. You might have noticed that we start at Chapter 10 and work our way to Chapter 0 – when you will be ready to 'go live' and step into your spotlight. You will also notice the TV-themed chapter titles – many inspired by shows I have worked on.

- ◊ **Real stories, real people:** You will find insights from a wide range of celebrity presenters and performers. They have either generously shared their personal stories with me or have spoken publicly about their confidence struggles. Many are people you will recognise, and some have since become good friends.

- ◊ **Client case studies:** I have also included anonymised examples from real clients I have worked with in my hypnotherapy practice. These stories show how confidence can grow and shift in the most surprising ways.

◊ **Practical exercises:** This book is packed with confidence-boosting exercises you can explore at your own pace. Look out for the **_Take Five_** moments and take time to pause and reflect on your progress.

◊ **Exclusive freebies:** As a 'Thank You' for picking up a copy of this book, I have created some special guided resources to support you on your journey towards stronger self-belief and lasting confidence. Simply scan the QR codes to access the guided content.

At the back of the book there are suggestions for further reading, other helpful resources and contact details.

Sprinkled throughout are a selection of behind-the-scenes celebrity tales – because, let's be honest, who doesn't want to know what really happens when the cameras stop rolling?

And a quick heads-up...

I will _try_ to avoid any unnecessary name-dropping as I share my stories, because no one likes a bragger! However, the stories will make much more sense if you know who they're from!

Like the BBC's mission statement, my hope is that this book will **inform, educate and entertain** – while giving you the tools to think, feel and act with greater confidence.

You have made a commitment to change, and I am here to support you every step of the way.

TAKE FIVE:

Before you start, make a note of where you think your confidence level is right now.

0 = Zero confidence

to

10 = Maximum confidence

Now ask yourself where would you like the level to be? Does this feel doable?

When you get to the end of the book, I will ask you to check your confidence level again and remind you to come back to see where you started. I am certain you will be happy with your progress!

You've got this!

With confidence,

Introduction

Confidence is the holy grail of the coaching and self-development world. And the industry built around it? A gold mine! Every year, it generates billions in revenue. Books, experts, apps, podcasts, masterclasses, retreats, YouTube tutorials – everywhere you look, someone is promising the fast-track to Confidence Town.

Q: So why on earth do we need another book about confidence?

Well, maybe you have already read a few of those books. Maybe you downloaded the app, took the course, followed the Insta expert, and yet you still haven't quite experienced the transformation you had hoped for.

Or maybe it all felt so overwhelming and confusing that you didn't know where to start. So, you didn't.

If that is the case, you are not alone.

I have read the books too. I have watched the videos and attended the masterclasses. I did all that to make sure this book offers something different.

You see, I have spent the past forty years helping people build real-world confidence, in my capacity as both a TV producer and hypnotherapist. Now I want to help you unlock yours. Not by promising overnight miracles, but by giving you practical, tested tools and strategies that work. My approach is grounded in experience, shaped by insight, and designed to meet you exactly where you are.

Confidence changes lives and I would love to help it change yours.

Q: What exactly is Confidence?

The textbook definition: Confidence is the belief and assurance that you can trust your own abilities (that's self-confidence) or the abilities of others. In simple terms, it is believing you can do something – even when it is difficult – and having the courage to try.

That sounds pretty straightforward, so why does it feel so hard to achieve? And how come other people make it look so easy?

That is the illogicality of confidence!

Q: What is different about this book?

I have had the unique opportunity to explore confidence from two very different – but equally valuable – perspectives:

◇ As a **multi-award-winning TV producer**, working closely with celebrities, presenters and everyday people on camera.

◊ As a **cognitive behavioural hypnotherapist**, helping clients manage anxiety, improve performance and rediscover their inner strength.

This book brings those two worlds together. It blends behind-the-scenes lessons from thirty-eight years in television with practical, evidence-based techniques from cognitive behavioural hypnotherapy (CBH).

CBH is a proven, effective therapeutic process. It blends cognitive behavioural therapy (CBT) and hypnosis to help change unhelpful thoughts and behaviours, build confidence and reinforce positive change at a deeper level.

Please do not feel nervous about the idea of 'hypnosis'. I know that word can be off-putting to some people, but there is nothing in this book that will trick your subconscious into doing anything against your will. That is not how hypnotherapy works. I promise that you won't start clucking like a chicken! You are in control – always.

This book provides you with all the essential skills, techniques and insights you need to assemble a valuable 'confidence toolkit' which will come in handy at every stage of your life.

And like all good books, this one is full of stories...starting with my own.

My story: Part 1

When I was a child, I loved being the centre of attention. Whether it was middle child syndrome or my dad's natural entertainer genes coming through, I was always at the front of the queue when the spotlight was up for grabs.

Some might say I was 'annoying'. I prefer 'endearing'.

I couldn't tell you how many backyard extravaganzas I wrote, directed, starred in, and forced my long-suffering family and neighbours to sit through! Despite my limited talent, they clapped dutifully, and for years, I assumed everyone loved being the centre of attention, like I did.

Looking back, I realise how lucky I was. I grew up in a home filled with unconditional love, where I had the freedom to try, fail, learn and try again, without fear of judgment. That freedom helped me develop something many people never get: a core of self-belief.

Of course, everyone has a different start in life, but no matter your past, it is never too late to rewrite your confidence story.

That doesn't mean I haven't had my own wobbles.

I still carry the emotional scars of my failed figure-skating career (I couldn't even stand up in the changing room), and I am definitely still not over being rejected from the Scout and Guide Gang Show. Yet, through school and university, my core confidence held steady.

It wasn't until I joined the BBC that I saw how wide the confidence spectrum really is!

Suddenly I was working with household names and A-List celebrities, some with confidence levels that were OFF THE SCALE! Working on shows like **Going Live!** and **Live & Kicking** gave me a front-row seat to watch how the pros prepared.

> *I like to think I was a bit like the great **Sir David Attenborough** – but I was observing soap stars and boy bands instead of gorillas and penguins!*

Some celebs were the same off camera as on. Others were totally different. I saw people who were nervous, shy, sometimes even sweating with fear – but the minute the red light on the camera went on, they switched it on! Then, as soon as the red light went off, they would visibly deflate.

It was fascinating to watch. These professionals knew how to psyche themselves up, deliver a brilliant performance and then revert to their shy, quiet, natural selves. I didn't realise it at the time, but those insights would become invaluable to me later on when I began teaching similar skills to clients in a therapy setting.

> *I help my clients achieve long–lasting change, rather than something you can only sustain for an hour or so.*

During my thirty-eight years at the BBC, I travelled the world and worked with everyone from Hollywood royalty to *actual* Royalty! However, I didn't just work with established performers and celebrities. I particularly enjoyed helping new presenters find their feet and supporting members of the public to feel more at ease in front of the camera.

And what I learned is this: **Confidence is not fixed**. It shifts and changes, and the good news is that you can learn to control it.

Once you understand how it works – how to think, feel and act more confidently – a whole new world of opportunities opens up!

If you have ever felt intimidated by how confident people appear on TV, here is the secret: even the most confident people experience nerves and self-doubt. The difference is that experienced performers have learned how to manage their inner dialogue and how to channel nervous energy in a way that enhances their performance, not sabotages it.

When researching for this book, I interviewed several celebrities I have worked with over the years. Their stories are candid, generous and refreshingly honest. Interestingly, many of them wished they'd had this kind of guidance when they were starting out. It would have saved them from having to learn the hard way!

My story: Part 2

These days, I am a cognitive behavioural hypnotherapist and the founder of **Silverbrook Hypnotherapy**. I specialise in helping people overcome confidence-related issues using a combination of techniques from my TV background, my therapy training and the world of hypnosis.

If you have ever looked into hypnotherapy, you will know that there are many different approaches. I chose cognitive behavioural hypnotherapy (CBH) because it matched the logic of my factual TV brain. It is grounded in the CBT principle that your thoughts (cognitions), feelings and behaviours are interconnected. Change one of these and the others follow.

CBH does not require you to delve endlessly into your past, looking for the traumatic trigger which 'caused' your issues. Instead, CBH starts with where you are now and focuses on moving forward, towards the goal you want to achieve.

Hypnotherapy is proven to be a safe, quick and effective way of tackling issues like anxiety, public speaking fears, social confidence, exam nerves...and much more!

And confidence expertise is the precise sweet spot, where the experience from both sides of my career overlap!

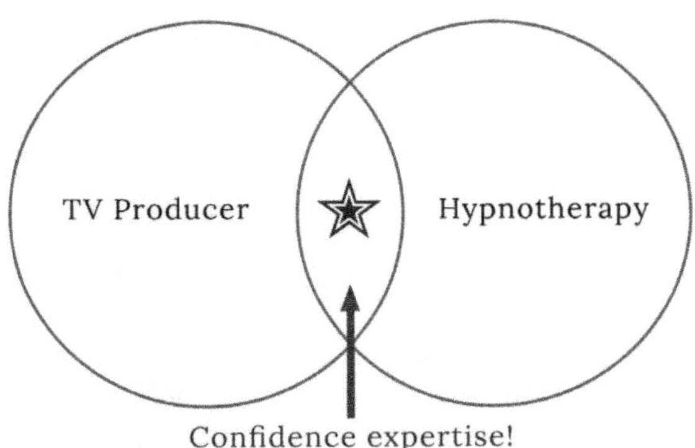

Confidence expertise!

Research indicates that up to 75% of people experience a fear of public speaking (glossophobia). That is a huge number, and I never underestimate the significant impact that kind of fear can have on both your personal and professional life.

But the good news is that you don't have to just live with it.

The exercises and techniques in this book are designed to help you manage those nerves and build real confidence from the inside out.

Soon, that job interview or big presentation won't feel quite so daunting!

If any of this sounds familiar, and if you recognise your own struggles in these pages, then you are in the right place.

 **TOMORROW'S WORLD:**

Before you go any further, take a moment to reflect and ask yourself – What would I like to achieve by the end of the book?

What is your end goal?

Consider how motivated you are to change. What will be different about your life when you feel more confident? Start to imagine and visualise how that would feel.

The best way to measure success is to identify your goal at the outset and then you can gauge whether you have achieved (or exceeded) your expectations.

And success in one area often leads to success in another.

So, are you ready to start? Then let's begin...

10

Here's One I Made Earlier

When you are developing a new TV series, you are competing for viewers alongside all the other TV shows on all the other platforms. Inventing a memorable catchphrase can help your show stand out from all the rest.

If you are lucky, that catchphrase will be absorbed into everyday use, and when you hear it being repeated back to you, you know your show has made an impact!

Catchphrases on my 'most-used' list are:

◊   'Computer says No.' – **Little Britain**

◊   'What's occurin'?' – **Gavin & Stacey**

◊   'Say what you see.' – **Catchphrase**

◊   'PIVOT!' – **Friends**

◊   'Back of the net!' – **Alan Partridge**

and, of course, the iconic...

◊   'Here's one I made earlier.' – **Blue Peter**

Blue Peter started broadcasting on 16 October 1958 and remains the world's longest-running children's TV programme. It is a national institution, and rightly so. For over six decades, it has given children a platform, a voice, and has helped achieve positive change to life in Britain and beyond!

As well as the show's legacy over its six+ decades, *Blue Peter* was ahead of its time in terms of new production techniques too. When you are broadcasting live for just thirty minutes, it is simply not possible to show every step of a Christmas cookie bake or a craft project, like making a replica of Tracy Island, in real-time. So, the team developed a workaround: demonstrate the start of a process, then unveil the finished result with the now-iconic line: *Here's one I made earlier.*

I was proud to nurture *Blue Peter*'s legacy in my role as executive producer for BBC Children's Factual Programmes, but having responsibility for this beloved brand was daunting. *Blue Peter* is the source of surprisingly passionate debates in some very senior circles!

> *A fun dinner party game I like to play is: Tell me who your Blue Peter presenters were and I'll guess your age!*
>
> *(FYI – mine were **John Noakes, Peter Purves** and **Valerie Singleton**.)*

As a 1970s viewer, I was very disappointed to find that sticky -backed plastic wasn't readily available in Cardiff, but I would never have imagined that, forty+ years later, one of my career highlights was to be awarded Blue Peter's highest accolade – the Gold *Blue Peter* badge!

Everyone who appears on the show receives the standard blue and white Blue Peter badge. Some celebs, like musician **Ed Sheeran** and Olympian **Sky Brown**, have even had the honour of designing a badge! But, to get the full *Blue Peter* experience, they also need to utter the immortal words: *Here's one I made earlier!*

Q: Congratulations on your Gold badge, Annette, but what does all this have to do with confidence?

A: Everything!

Because *Here's one I made earlier* is the ultimate metaphor for preparation.

Why preparation matters

Every celebrity I interviewed for this book agreed that preparation is the single most powerful tool in your confidence kit.

> ## "I have never been someone who gets a thrill from flying by the seat of my pants!"
>
> Michelle Ackerley

And it matters even more when you are in the spotlight. Just ask **Ortis Deley** about his *disastrous stint at Channel 4*.

In 2011, Ortis hosted Channel 4's live coverage of the **World Athletics Championships**. A talented presenter known for his wit and warmth, Ortis's comfort zone is on live TV. However, that day, something was off. He stumbled, lost his place, and struggled to recover. Millions of viewers noticed.

What went wrong?

He hadn't prepared properly. He had skipped the golden rule:

Confidence Rule #1:

Never shortcut the preparation process.

To his credit, Ortis didn't let this derail his career. He reflected, adapted and rebuilt – but now he always insists on doing all of his own research!

His advice: *Ask questions. Do your homework. Know your subject. Never rely on someone else to prep for you.*

"I do my own research. If something's wrong in those notes, it's my responsibility. Preparation is what gives me confidence."

Angellica Bell

Sally Gray MBE learned a similar lesson, but hers happened during her schooldays. At age ten, Sally stood onstage, in front of her Edinburgh classmates, to recite a poem she had learned diligently. Halfway through, Sally froze! Despite weeks of practice, the words evaporated. Why? Because she had memorised the poem without fully understanding it.

Both Sally and Ortis learned this lesson the hard way, but once learned, it can set you up for success. Now, Sally and Ortis always make time to prepare.

> ## "It's good to learn from your mistakes. It's better to learn from other people's mistakes."
>
> Warren Buffet

Q: How do you prepare for confidence?

I am asked this question a lot and I assume, as you are currently reading this book, that you would like to know the answer too.

Let's first debunk a few popular misconceptions with a quick general knowledge exercise:

CONFIDENCE: TRUE or FALSE?

1. ***Confident people are always the loudest voice in the room.*** TRUE / FALSE

   True confidence does not need to shout. It communicates with clarity and presence.

2. ***Only extroverts can be confident.*** TRUE / FALSE

   Introverts can be just as confident; they simply recharge differently. (Michelle Ackerley, Jamie Theakston and Ricky Wilson are great examples of confident introverts.)

3. ***Confident people don't feel nervous.*** TRUE / FALSE

   Everyone feels nerves and self-doubt. Confidence is about how you handle those feelings.

4. ***Confidence is something you are born with.*** TRUE / FALSE

   Confidence is a skill, and like any skill, it can be learned.

5. ***It is harder to become confident as you get older*** TRUE / FALSE

   Life experience can help you build deeper, more lasting confidence. There is no expiry date!

OK, it wasn't much of a True or False quiz, as all the answers were FALSE, but how did you do? Are you feeling more optimistic about your chance of success?

TAKE FIVE:

When you were answering those questions, did any particular people spring to mind? Are any of these people who came to mind helpful role models, with self-confidence levels you would like to emulate? Or alternatively, are their behaviours not ones you want to mimic?

If you are having a crisis of confidence, it can be helpful to have your role model in mind and ask: *What would X do?* Then...do that!

> *I have a sign in my downstairs toilet which poses a very important question: What would **Elvis** do?*
>
> *That's not bad advice to consider, unless you are trying to break away from your unhealthy eating habits or have an aversion to bejewelled jumpsuits!*

 **Krishnan Guru-Murthy: Do Your Homework** 

I have known **Krishnan Guru-Murthy** since 1991, when we first worked together on the BBC Children's daily news programme, **Newsround**.

My first impression of Krishnan was that he was the epitome of 'confidence'. He was twenty-one, had just finished his philosophy, politics and economics degree at Oxford, had a brilliantly inquisitive mind, had already been a TV presenter for three years and he drove a red Mazda MX5. (I also remember that the annual insurance premium on that car was extortionate!)

He was the co-host of *Newsround* (alongside my flat-mate, **Juliet Morris**) and to me, he seemed completely fearless. In truth, some people thought Krishnan was veering more towards the cocky/arrogant side, but his overall level of confidence was undeniable.

Krishnan told me that in his early years, confidence came easily, but as he grew older, he recognised the importance of preparation: *As that innate confidence of youth falls away, and you realise how little you know, you make up for it by being prepared and gaining knowledge.*

Early on, Krishnan studied the likes of **David Dimbleby** and **Jeremy Paxman**, learning by observation and meticulous critique. He then used these insights to build the framework for his own style, rooted in diligent prep and reflective learning.

His advice?

When you're faced with something unfamiliar, stop and think. Read, ask questions, watch others, learn everything you can. Then you can make informed decisions. That gives you confidence.

This thorough, considered approach has kept Krishnan grounded through tough interviews and even warzone reporting. But in 2023, he faced a very different confidence challenge: **Strictly Come Dancing.**

More on how Krishnan coped when he swapped his suits and flak jackets for sequins and spandex, in Chapter 4 – It'll be Alright on the Night.

Upskill: Self-Hypnosis for Confidence

Self-hypnosis is usually one of the first coping techniques I teach my clients because it acts as a gentle introduction to the experience. (Technically, all hypnosis is self-hypnosis, because you cannot hypnotise someone against their will.)

Being in control of the process reassures them that they won't feel uncomfortable. It is also a surprisingly versatile and valuable life skill.

> *I often use self-hypnosis to help me zone out at the dentist or when I'm having difficulty falling asleep!*

In simple terms, self-hypnosis is a focused state of calm awareness. It allows you to block out distracting thoughts, so that your mind can fully focus on more positive and helpful suggestions.

Like any skill, the more you practise, the easier it becomes. If you can spend five to ten minutes doing this every day, you will soon notice the benefits.

Note: As previously mentioned, if you have a serious mental health issue, please seek advice from your doctor. There are some conditions where hypnosis is not recommended.

EXERCISE: FIVE MINUTE SELF-HYPNOSIS

Use this exercise daily to prepare for any situation where you want to feel more confident. Please scan the QR code if you would like me to guide you through this exercise.

Step 1: Get comfortable

Find a quiet spot where you feel safe. Sit with your feet flat on the floor, hands in your lap. Close your eyes.

Step 2: Focus on your breath

Inhale deeply through your nose. Exhale slowly through your mouth. Repeat three times. Let your shoulders drop. Scan your body for any areas of tension and release it.

Step 3: Countdown to calm

Silently count down from ten to one. With each number, imagine sinking deeper into a calm, relaxed state. At one, picture a peaceful place where you feel capable and safe. Use all your senses to make it feel as vivid and real as possible.

Step 4: Positive rehearsal

Visualise the situation you are preparing for. See yourself standing tall, speaking clearly, feeling steady. Let the success play out in your mind.

Step 5: Affirm your confidence

Repeat silently: *I am calm, capable and confident.* Say it three times with intention.

Step 6: Return and reconnect

When you are ready, count from one to five, telling yourself that you are coming back, feeling refreshed and ready. Open your eyes and have a good stretch. Notice how much steadier and clearer you feel.

TAKE FIVE: 

While this exercise is still fresh in your mind, jot down a few notes, reflecting on how it felt:

◊ Did you notice any areas of tension in your body? If so, where?

◊ What thoughts (if any) popped into your head? How did you respond to those thoughts?

◊ Where was your peaceful place? Did you really feel as if you were there?

◊ Which of your senses was the most vivid? e.g. sight, smell.

◊ How did you feel when you were saying: *I am calm, capable and confident?*

◊ Did you notice anything else which surprised you?

Having a note of your observations will allow you to compare your progress, because self-hypnosis gets easier with practice. You can always return to your peaceful place and give yourself a confidence boost, whenever you need to!

KEY TAKEAWAY:

Confidence doesn't start on the stage or in the spotlight. It starts in the preparation. Whether you are speaking in public, tackling a new challenge, or just trying something new, a confident performance begins long before anyone is watching.

So do the work. Prepare. Make one earlier!

Well done! You have finished Chapter 10. But before you turn the page, please pause and make sure that you have absorbed everything you have learned so far.

Reflection Question:

Which of the techniques or ideas in this chapter feels most relevant to me right now, and how can I begin to apply it?

You can use your notebook or this space to jot down any thoughts or reflections.

When you are ready... let's move on!

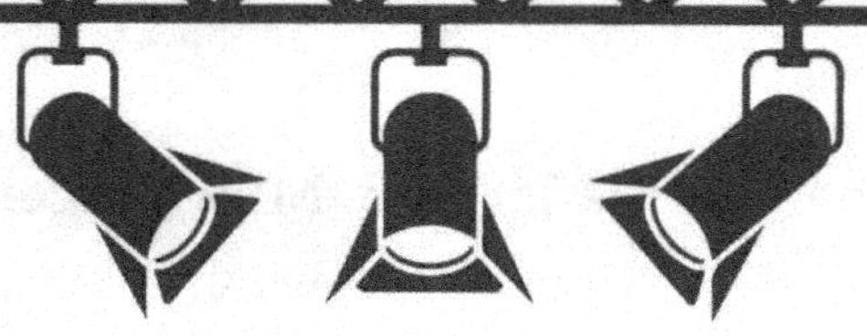

9

It'll Never Work?

It'll Never Work? was one of my all-time favourite series to produce. This ground-breaking, multi-award-winning science and technology show for BBC Children's took me around the world for six unforgettable summers. I had the privilege of filming extraordinary stories of human creativity, meeting pioneers who proved the doubters wrong, and learning that when someone says *It'll never work*, it might just mean that you are onto something.

> *I know the title might not win any grammar awards, but we added the question mark deliberately. It helped smooth things over when negotiating with big organisations like NASA and Nike, who might otherwise have worried we were criticising their inventions.*
>
> *I think they chalked it up to British eccentricity!*

Imagine if **Alexander Graham Bell** (telephone), **Marie Curie** (radioactivity) or **Charles Babbage** (computer) had taken *It'll never work* to heart? The world would be a very different place.

The INW? presenters – **Sally Gray MBE**, **Angela Lamont**, and **Rick Adams** – were curious, fearless and smart. Believe me, some of the location filming setups required super-human levels of confidence, so I am eternally grateful to all of them.

> *One personal low point I remember from an INW? shoot, was when we were in Tokyo, filming an item about innovative Japanese toilet design. As the director, I wanted a specific shot of this unique technology...so I found myself lying on the floor of a urinal, wearing what transpired to be a very absorbent T-shirt!*
>
> *That top was never seen again!*

From Invention to Intervention

It'll Never Work? is also the perfect title for this chapter, because it introduces one of the biggest blocks to confidence: **Thinking Errors.**

Thinking errors are subconscious patterns of negative or distorted thoughts. Often, we don't even realise we are doing it, but these mental bad habits shape how we interpret the world and can seriously undermine our self-belief.

You may know someone who always approaches everything with a 'glass half empty' attitude. Maybe that someone is you? This is just one example of how a negative mental filter can skew your perception.

But here is the empowering truth, and possibly the most important thing to take away from this book:

Confidence Rule #2:

YOU are in control of your thoughts. Your thoughts do NOT control you.

When you understand this fundamental truth, you reclaim the power to change the way you think, feel and behave.

So, I think it is time to identify your Thinking Errors with a quick quiz.

> *I love magazine quizzes like 'Which Sex in the City character are you?'*
>
> *Hopefully, I am not the only person who repeats the quiz until you get the answer you want!*
>
> *It's Carrie, of course!*

Let's find out which thinking errors might be affecting you.

EXERCISE: WHAT ARE YOUR THINKING ERRORS?

Instructions: Note the option that feels most like your usual reaction in each situation. Don't overthink it, just go with your gut.

1. You make a small mistake at work. What goes through your mind?

A. That's it. I've ruined everything. I'll probably get fired.

B. I always mess things up. I'm just not good enough.

C. I either do this perfectly or I'm a total failure.

D. Ugh, why am I so stupid?

E. This one mistake proves I can't handle pressure.

F. It's just a small mistake. I can fix it and move on.

2. Your friend doesn't text you back for a few days. What do you assume?

A. They must be angry with me.

B. They probably hate me now.

C. If they cared about me, they'd reply right away.

D. I must've done something wrong. Typical me!

E. This always happens. No one really sticks around.

F. They're probably just busy. It's nothing personal.

3. You get a compliment but feel awkward. What do you think?

A. They're just being polite.

B. They don't really mean it.

C. One compliment doesn't mean anything. I'm still not good enough.

D. They clearly don't know the real me.

E. They must want something from me.

F. That was kind of them. I'll just say thank you.

4. You try something new, and it doesn't go well. How do you react?

A. What if this means I'll never succeed at anything?

B. I am a total failure.

C. I am either great at things or totally useless, there's no in-between.

D. I have embarrassed myself. Everyone's judging me.

E. I should've known better than to even try.

F. That didn't work out, but I can learn from it.

5. You are preparing for a presentation. What is your inner voice saying?

A. If I mess up, it will be a disaster.

B. I'm terrible at this stuff.

C. If I don't do this perfectly, it will be a total failure.

D. I know I'll say something stupid.

E. I'm not cut out for things like this.

F. I might feel nervous, but I've prepared well, and I can do this.

Now count how many times you picked each letter to find out which thinking errors you are most likely to make – or whether you tend to avoid them altogether.

No cheating by peeking at the results first!

RESULTS

Mostly A = Catastrophising

You tend to expect the worst-case scenario and mentally snowball small issues into huge disasters.

Mostly B = Labelling

You attach negative labels to yourself quickly, like 'loser' or 'failure'.

Mostly C = Black and White or All or Nothing Thinking

You see things in extremes – something is either perfect or awful, a success or failure.

Mostly D = Personalisation

You assume others are judging you or that you are the cause of things going wrong.

Mostly E = Overgeneralisation

You make sweeping conclusions based on one event, e.g. *This always happens!*

Mostly F = Balanced Thinking

You tend to interpret situations more neutrally or realistically, without jumping to unhelpful conclusions.

TAKE FIVE:

So, what have you learned? Can you recognise some of these habits in your thought patterns? Do some of the A - E responses sound like you? You might be a mixture of a few or even a little bit of all of them!

If your quiz results suggest that you are a doomed loser who thinks that *whatever* you do, it is going to end up as a disaster, and you are entirely to blame, please don't worry!

The fact that you are reading this means you are ready to change your self-belief. And more good news? These thought patterns can be challenged and changed.

Rewriting the script – Your Inner Critic

We all have an 'inner critic', that little voice inside our head that can be quick to point out our flaws, question our abilities or predict the worst. It often develops as a way of trying to keep us safe from mistakes, rejection or embarrassment, but instead of being helpful, it usually holds us back.

Your inner critic might sound like: *You'll mess this up, Everyone is judging you*, or *You're not good enough*. The key thing to remember is that this voice is not the truth – it is just a habit of thinking. By learning to notice it, challenge it and replace it with more balanced self-talk, you can quieten that critic and give more airtime to your supportive, encouraging inner voice instead.

Think of your inner critic like a grumpy backseat passenger who keeps second-guessing your driving. They are noisy and distracting, but they don't actually have their hands on the wheel! However, if you keep hearing the same negative mantra on an internal loop, then you are increasing the odds of it coming true. However, the more often you interrupt these patterns, the weaker they become.

Ask yourself: *Would I speak to my friend the way I talk to myself?* If not, it is time to rewrite the script and reprogramme your satnav.

Why your brain expects danger

Our brains are hard-wired with a 'negativity bias'. This comes from evolution: thousands of years ago, being alert to danger – like spotting a predator or remembering which plants made us sick – kept us alive. Missing a positive moment wasn't risky, but missing a threat could be fatal.

The most common reflex to a perceived threat is the **fight-or-flight** response.

Your fight-or-flight response is pre-programmed, so even though we are unlikely to face a lion on the way to work, our brain still scans for problems, criticism or mistakes first. It's not that you are overly negative – it is simply your survival system doing its job.

The good news is, with practice, you can train your brain to notice the positives more often and balance out that bias.

Q: How can you override these automatic responses?

1. The first step is simply to notice when you are having an unhelpful thought – to catch yourself in the moment. Our thoughts don't just stay in our heads, they directly influence how we feel emotionally and how we act in response.

For example, if you think, *I'm going to mess this up*, you might start to feel anxious, and that anxiety could lead you to avoid the task or rush through it nervously.

On the other hand, recognizing the thought for what it is – just a thought, not a fact – gives you the chance to pause and choose a different response. By becoming aware of this chain reaction between thoughts, feelings and behaviours, you can begin to break old patterns and create more helpful ones.

2. The next step is to practise the breathing technique you learned in the previous chapter:

    ◊ Take a deep breath in through your nose...and slowly exhale through your mouth.

    ◊ Repeat this three times.

    ◊ Let your shoulders drop and your jaw relax.

Alternatively, the Box Breathing technique is also very effective:

    ◊ Inhale through your nose for the count of four – 1 2 3 4

    ◊ Hold for the count of four – 1 2 3 4

    ◊ Exhale gently for the count of four – 1 2 3 4

    ◊ Pause for the count of four – 1 2 3 4

This enables your parasympathetic nervous system to kick in.

The parasympathetic nervous system is the part of your body's 'rest and digest' response. It works like a natural brake after stress, slowing your heart rate, lowering blood pressure and helping your body return to balance. When it is active, you feel calmer, more grounded and better able to think clearly – the opposite of the fight-or-flight state triggered by the sympathetic nervous system.

3. Observe how you are feeling and behaving. Understand the real impact this thought is having on you.

   Then, objectively consider a different perspective on the situation. Is there another, more helpful way to interpret it?

   For example, try **these alternative suggestions**.

   If you are prone to:

   ◊ **Catastrophisation** – the *That's it, I've ruined everything, I'll probably get fired*-type response.

     Recognise that your mind is racing into the future and bring yourself back to the present. Then, focus on the most likely, not the scariest outcome.

     Ask yourself: *Am I jumping to the worst-case scenario? What is the most likely outcome?*

   ◊ **Labelling** – the *I always mess things up, I'm just not good enough*-type response.

     Try replacing labels with facts: *I made a mistake* rather than *I am a mistake.*

> *I worked with a client who described herself as being 'so clumsy'. When I asked what the last 'clumsy' thing was she had done, she couldn't remember!*
>
> *It was just a label which had stuck.*

◊ **Black or White/All or Nothing thinking** – the *If I don't do this perfectly, it will be a total failure*-type response.

Practise finding the grey/middle ground: *It wasn't ideal, but it wasn't a disaster either.* Always note the positive feedback, lessons or outcomes too.

◊ **Personalisation** – the *I must've done something wrong, typical me*-type response.

Challenge those assumptions. What actual evidence supports that thought?

Don't assume responsibilities for things which are outside your control.

◊ **Overgeneralisation** – the *This always happens*-type response.

Try narrowing your thoughts to this specific moment/incident: *This happened today, not always.*

Just because you weren't successful on this occasion, it doesn't mean you won't be in the future.

Practising any new habit takes time, but the more you repeat these steps, the more your brain will adjust to the new positive programming. Keep persevering until this becomes your new default setting.

This is when a **Thought Diary** can come in handy.

EXERCISE: KEEP A THOUGHT DIARY

Use this Thought Diary to note the triggers and impact of any negative feelings. Then consider what would be a more helpful, realistic or positive response.

An example scenario: Imagine this situation – your boss has just asked you to take on some of the workload from a colleague who is underperforming. Notice how you immediately react to this request. Perhaps it is something like: *Why is it always me? I am the only person here who does any work! Why do they employ people who aren't up to the job?* Once you have noted your reflex response, use these prompts to critique your thoughts, feeling and behaviours in more detail. You can note your observations on page 45.

What thoughts are going through your mind?

◊   How does this request make you feel?

◊   Are you experiencing any new or strong emotions?

◊   Do you notice any changes to how your body feels?

◊ Do you notice any changes to your behaviour after you were asked to help vs the way you were behaving before the conversation with your boss?

Then in the last column, consider an alternative thought or explanation as to why the boss asked you to do this extra work. For example, *I know that there's a fixed deadline to complete this work. If we miss it, we risk losing their business. If that happens, then everyone's job will be at risk. So, my boss's priority is to complete the job before the deadline, and I am the most experienced member of the team.*

Notice the difference? Same situation but very different thoughts, feelings and behaviours.

I suggest you use the Thought Diary for a full week, as this will allow you to spot any patterns and get used to seeing situations from a different perspective.

You can use this template in the book or your journal to note down the specific details.

Day	Situation/ What happened?	Unhelpful thoughts?	Emotions or sensations?	Behaviour?	Alternative thoughts

TAKE FIVE:

Do you notice any patterns emerging? What can you learn from your observations? Notice how your thoughts, feelings and behaviours are all inter-connected. Awareness is the first step to change.

Remember:

YOU ARE IN CONTROL OF YOUR THOUGHTS.

Client Case Study: William

William had been in his current role for ten years when there was an opportunity for a promotion. He had the required skills and the support of his current boss, but a loop of catastrophic thoughts paralysed him. In his mind, *if* he took the job, everything would unravel. He would fail, get fired, be unable to return to his former role, and his career would spiral downward.

These thoughts triggered panic attacks.

Over five sessions, we worked on challenging these predictions, grounding him in facts, and learning self-soothing skills. These included calming breathing methods, techniques to minimise the impact of unhelpful and distracting thoughts and how to prevent catastrophisation by grounding his mind and body in the present moment.

Hypnosis enabled William to mentally rehearse and experience thriving in this new role, therefore removing the fear of the unknown.

The result? William applied and he got the job! The bonus is that he now has a selection of tools he can utilise to manage his stress levels and to assess situations more realistically for the rest of his life

William learned to recognise that the catastrophic scenarios he had imagined existed only in his head. Once he had the techniques to keep any unhelpful thoughts under control, his confidence levels increased. This enabled him to properly assess his options and make a balanced and informed decision as to what he wanted to do next.

William still needs to keep practising, as old patterns don't vanish overnight.

But the belief that he can change? That has been transformative.

 **Les Dennis: Try Swapping Shoes** 

I had the pleasure of working with **Les Dennis** on the fantasy game show *Fee Fi Fo Yum*. The premise was that Les, playing 'TV gameshow host extraordinaire – Les Dennis' was captured by a giant and forced to host a deadly gameshow, where the losing team of children were eaten by said giant! There could possibly have been a beanstalk and perhaps a massive goose involved too…but I really can't remember!

Les admits his nerves have increased with age but so has his wisdom: *You learn to live through it.* However, when preparing for a particularly stressful stage role, he turned to renowned hypnotist **Paul McKenna** for help with some positive visualisation to combat his nerves:

As press night approached, I got more anxious and had a huge fear of bad reviews. Paul (McKenna) was amazing and took me through some great techniques to help me get through my performance.

*He asked me to visualise an actor I admired, then asked me to imagine his shoes in front of me and then to step into them. Literally, to STEP INTO HIS SHOES! I chose the multi-award-winning actor **Anthony Hopkins**. This simple and effective visualisation technique got me through press night, and the show reviews were great!*

I've learnt that a few nerves every time are to be expected, but they will dissipate as soon as I walk on stage.

In fact, I hope I keep on having stage fright, because nerves are a sign that you care, but I now have the techniques to keep them under control.

 **Ted Robbins: Believe in Yourself** 

Another entertainment veteran (and I know he won't mind me calling him that) is **Ted Robbins**.

For some, Ted might be best known for his comedy roles in TV shows like *Phoenix Nights* and *Benidorm*, but for a generation of children, Ted will forever be 'The Governor' from *The Slammer*. The white-suited custodian of guilty performers who have committed crimes against showbusiness.

Ted is part of a showbiz dynasty, so he knows a few things! His first cousin (once removed) is **Sir Paul McCartney**, his dad was an important early mentor for **John Lennon** and (nephew) Paul. Ted's sister **Kate Robbins** is in the business, as is his niece **Emily Atack**.

Ted has worked alongside some of the British comedy greats, including **Bob Monkhouse**, **Les Dawson**, **Peter Kay** and **Des O'Connor**, and he is a fantastic raconteur.

> *If you ever get the chance, I highly recommend time spent with Ted Robbins, as he reminisces about his extensive and very entertaining career.*

Ted's advice for keeping any fears and negative thoughts in perspective is to *remember that you've been invited to do this* (speech, performance, interview, presentation...whatever) *because you're good at what you do!*

Breathe deeply, smile and always remember that what you do is just a small part of who you are. Some days you'll win and some days you won't win, but be confident, be brave and hopefully you'll go home to someone who loves you.

Certainly, some wise words from 'The Governor' to reflect on at the end of this chapter.

 **KEY TAKEAWAY:**

Thinking errors are not facts. They are habits, and habits can be changed.

Use a Thought Diary to start noticing your patterns. Challenge your inner critic and replace fear with self-awareness.

That's how confidence is built – thought by thought.

That's Chapter 9 done! But before you go onto the next one, please take a moment to reflect and absorb everything you have learned so far.

How does this chapter challenge or confirm what you previously believed about confidence?

You can use your notebook or this space to jot down any helpful thoughts or reflections.

8

Master(your)Mind(set)

Ricky Wilson

Q: What is the biggest blocker to confidence?

A: It is not your skills or experience – it's the way you think!

Your mindset is the filter through which you experience the world. It is shaped by your upbringing, cultural background, beliefs absorbed from parents, teachers, peers and your own personal experiences. While it can evolve over time, some of the core beliefs that hold us back, like not feeling 'good enough', can be deeply embedded.

The good news? With the right tools, your mindset can be rewired.

Q: *What is the difference between thinking errors and mental mindsets?*

A: *In short, thinking errors are moment-to-moment slips in thinking, while mindsets are the long-term patterns that set the tone for how you think, feel and act.*

◊ **Thinking Errors** are specific, unhelpful thought patterns that distort reality in the moment. For example, *If I'm not perfect, I'm a complete failure* (all-or-nothing thinking) or *This always happens to me* (overgeneralisation). They are like mental 'glitches' – automatic and often exaggerated reactions to a situation.

◊ **Mental Mindsets**, on the other hand, are broader, more enduring attitudes or outlooks that shape how you approach life. For example, having a **fixed mindset**, e.g. *I can't change, I'm just not good at this*, versus a **growth mindset**, e.g. *I can learn and improve with effort.*

Mindsets are the 'lens' you see the world through, influencing your thoughts and behaviours over time.

 **Angellica Bell: The Power of Mindset** 

I have known Angellica for her entire broadcasting career – because I was the lucky executive producer who opened the package containing her CV and showreel! It was immediately clear she had something special, so I gave her the first of many presenting roles for BBC Children's. One of them was *K Club* on BBC Knowledge – a pioneering interactive show that also featured a fourteen-year-old **Marvin Humes** making his TV debut!

Over twenty-five years later, Angellica has become a stalwart of British television – from *CBBC* and *The One Show* to *Celebrity MasterChef* and *Big Brother*. But what makes her story so powerful isn't fame or longevity. It is her honesty about what it really takes to stay confident and grounded when all eyes are on you:

Sometimes how you perceive yourself – and how successful you think you are – isn't necessarily what other people see.

That self-awareness was forged during the early days of live TV – a high-pressure environment where mistakes happened in front of millions, and feedback came thick and fast.

I was completely out of my depth! One minute I was just Angellica, walking down the street with no one noticing me, and the next, everyone knew who I was. I remember watching myself back on screen and thinking, 'Who do I want to be? How do I want to be seen?' It was demoralising at times, but it taught me so much.

Angellica's story is a masterclass in mindset. Instead of letting critique crush her, she used it to build her confidence muscle: *I didn't let criticism break me − I used it to build me.*

That simple reframe changed everything. Rather than interpreting mistakes as failure, she saw them as data, as feedback, as part of the process.

You have to build a thick skin. There's nothing wrong with getting things wrong. You learn, you improve, you keep going.

Angellica's core confidence is rooted in self-belief, integrity, and the courage to stay authentic. Never one to shy away from a challenge, she initially turned down **Celebrity MasterChef**, despite being a great cook.

I was taught to cook by my grandmother, and it's something very personal to me. I wasn't sure I could do it because I didn't want to let her down.

Luckily, she reconsidered…and went on to win the whole contest!

Another vital component of Angellica's confidence toolkit is the support she surrounds herself with.

I've always had good people around me. Have people you trust. People who lift you, not plant doubt in you.

And her definition of confidence?

Confidence is that innate belief that you are capable of achieving anything. But it also comes from overcoming self-doubt. Everybody has it. The power comes from facing it and doing it anyway.

That's the essence of real confidence – not the glossy kind that looks perfect under studio lights, but the grounded kind that comes from knowing who you are.

Your Comfort, Growth and Danger Zones

It is important to understand that humans learn and evolve by moving purposefully between three different zones: Comfort, Growth and Danger.

These zones aren't physical places, they are **states of learning and emotional experience.**

◊　In the **Comfort Zone**, you feel safe and steady. It is emotionally reassuring but offers little challenge, so intellectual and personal development stay limited.

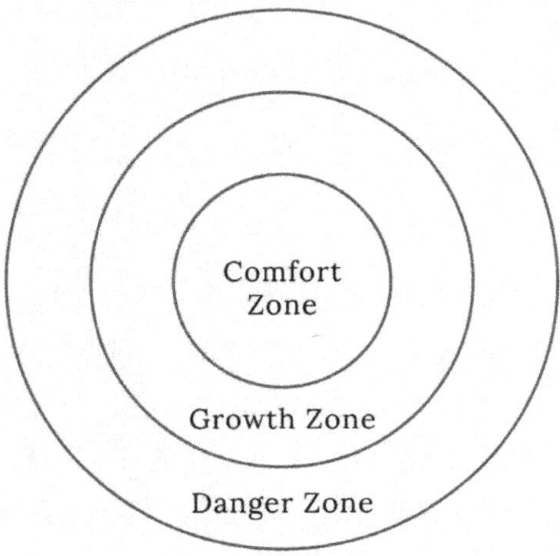

◇ In the **Growth Zone**, you experience some uncertainty and stretch, but in a manageable way. This balance of challenge and support stimulates both intellectual learning (new skills, problem-solving) and emotional growth (resilience, confidence).

◇ In the **Danger Zone**, the challenge feels overwhelming. Stress or fear hijacks your ability to learn or grow, so development is blocked rather than supported.

In short, these zones map how your mind and emotions respond to challenge – from safety to stretch to overwhelm. Real growth happens by stepping gently out of comfort, but not so far that we tip into danger.

TAKE FIVE:

Which zone do you spend most time in? Why do you think that is? Does this explain any of your thoughts, feelings or behaviours?

Don't forget that the human brain is hardwired to keep us safe. It sees danger lurking around every corner. So, there is nothing your brain likes more than knowing you are staying nice and safe in your Comfort Zone – and far, far away from the Danger Zone.

Of course, some people love the thrill of the Danger Zone and thrive on being far outside their Comfort Zone. But for most of us non-adrenaline junkies – and especially those with a natural risk-aversion – the thought of life in this outer zone can feel overwhelming.

However, this doesn't mean you have to stay stuck in the centre, because there is an important zone, between the Comfort Zone and the Danger Zone: the Growth Zone.

Moving into the Growth Zone still requires conscious effort, but it's much, much less scary.

Another benefit? Every time you push into the Growth Zone, your Comfort Zone expands. And as your Comfort Zone expands, the Growth Zone expands into what used to feel like the Danger Zone, therefore shrinking your fear.

Simply by taking regular, small steps into the Growth Zone and getting positive experiences of learning and development, the size and impact of the Danger Zone shrinks. So, something that once felt impossible becomes doable.

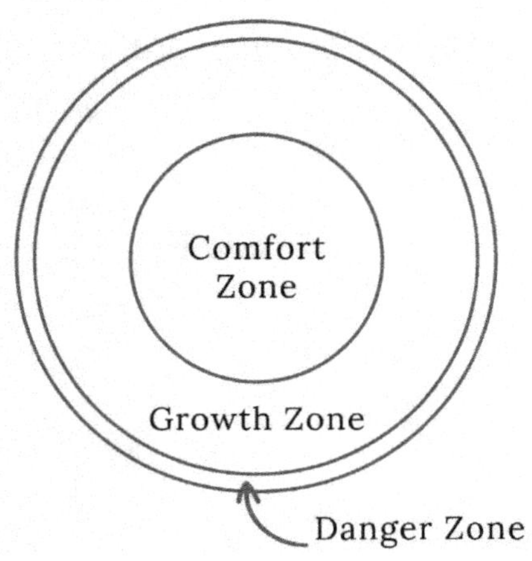

You still might not want to go free-diving or audition for *Britain's Got Talent*, but that becomes a conscious choice, not one made from fear.

Q: How do you move into the Growth Zone?

A: You need to master your mindset!

Ask yourself: Is it Nerves or Excitement?

Nerves and excitement trigger the same physical sensations: increased heart rate, fluttery stomach, sweaty palms. So, it is up to you to decide whether you are feeling anxious...or exhilarated.

> *Oh boy! I woefully underestimated the amount of advice my celebrity friends wanted to share about how they have learned to manage their mindset and reframe their nerves!*
>
> *They had to learn these lessons the hard way – but this book is your Golden Ticket to Confidence Town!*

Brace yourself...we're going in!

 # Helen Skelton: Fearless Focus 

When **Helen Skelton** became a *Blue Peter* presenter in 2008, 'stepping out of your comfort zone' could easily have been part of the job description. The bar had been set decades earlier by daredevil presenters like John Noakes, who famously scaled Nelson's Column without a safety harness, tackled the Cresta Run and even became the first civilian to complete a five-mile freefall parachute jump with the RAF.

So, for Helen, pushing boundaries wasn't optional, it was expected.

Her pragmatic approach to new challenges helped her keep everything in perspective during her five years on the show.

Most of life is a challenge. It constantly throws things at you that are new and you have no reference point for. On Blue Peter, that was sort of the job – trying things that put you completely out of your comfort zone.

Helen quickly earned a reputation as a fearless action-woman, inspiring a generation of young viewers. She didn't just do challenges, she conquered them. From walking a tightrope between the towers of Battersea Power Station to completing a 78-mile ultra-marathon in the Namibian desert, and from trekking 500 miles to the South Pole to kayaking 2,010 miles solo down the Amazon River – her many achievements redefined what was possible.

So how did she get into the right mindset to take on such extraordinary feats?

Perspective is everything, which is probably why I train for things. I like to go into something knowing I've prepared, and that, for me, is the ultimate confidence boost. It's about breaking it down and taking it one part at a time.

I never thought, 'Oh hang on, I have to walk on a high wire.' I literally thought, 'I just have to take three steps. Then a deep breath. Then three more.'

When I rowed the Amazon, I didn't think, 'I'm going to row the Amazon.' I thought, 'I know I can row 16 miles, so I'm going to do that loads of times.'

Over the years, Helen has learned to channel her energy for maximum focus.

I'm more of a frenetic energy kind of person. I don't think nerves are a bad thing, as long as you don't let them take over. Nerves are a sign that you care – and what's wrong with that? It's about reframing nerves and seeing them as a positive.

With a mindset like that, it is easy to see how Helen continues to thrive in whatever situation she finds herself in – with or without a kayak paddle in hand!

Helen's story is a reminder that confidence isn't about being fearless, it's about focusing on what works for you. And that is something Ricky Wilson has learned too…

 # Ricky Wilson: Persona vs Person 

Ricky Wilson is probably best known as the lead singer of the UK rock band *Kaiser Chiefs*. However, he is also a writer, radio presenter, TV host and artist, which is how we ended up working together.

We were gearing up to film a new CBBC series where talented young artists compete to win the title of *Britain's Best Young Artist*. Ricky, in his pre-rock star days, was an art lecturer at Leeds College of Art and Design, so he was the perfect choice to present the series, alongside his co-host, **Vick Hope**.

Then COVID hit.

Production stopped, and BBYA was put on hold for twelve months. But with Ricky stuck at home like the rest of us, we quickly developed a new show for him to host: *Ricky Wilson's Art Jam*. This series was a more manageable scale, in terms of the number of contributors involved and size of crew needed to film it.

They say that every cloud has a silver lining, and as it turned out, this stopgap series became the perfect warm-up act. Viewers got to know Ricky as an artist, not just a rock star, and by the time BBYA aired a year later, the audience was already on board.

Before I met Ricky, I *thought* I knew what to expect – a classic rock showman: outspoken, confident and a huge ego. But I was completely wrong.

Because 'Ricky', the swaggering frontman, is a persona, a character he created to survive and perform. (Real) Ricky is an introvert who finds groups exhausting. He needs quiet, solitude and time to gather his energy.

> *Being able to observe Ricky switch from introspective artist to fearless frontman made me re-evaluate everything I believed about confidence. It wasn't about having no fear, it was about knowing how to manage it.*

Ricky describes 'Ricky' as a *bit of a dick* and doubts they would even be friends in real life. But 'Ricky' is a brilliant coping mechanism.

As a child, Ricky was quiet and reserved, but when he got to Art School, he made a conscious decision to re-invent himself as an outgoing, attention-seeking extrovert. He just flicked a switch inside his brain and turned his confidence dial up to eleven.

Of course, presenting yourself as a high-energy, gregarious spotlight-seeker is exhausting, especially for a natural introvert. However, over the years, Ricky has become adept at switching his alter ego on and off.

'Ricky' is who Kaiser Chief fans want to see, but keeping up the façade has taken its toll on Ricky.

He is open about the therapy he has had to help manage the pressure. Ricky has learned how to channel nerves into excitement, and how to accept that fear, even after more than twenty years, never fully goes away:

I always go early to the stage, at least an hour or two beforehand – much to the annoyance of the rest of the band! I'm very quiet and I go very into myself. I pace a lot. I don't really like talking. I always feel sick.

But once I'm on stage, after ten seconds or so, it's fine. Then the other 'Ricky' takes over. The nerves never go away, but I recognise them now. I know they don't last. And I've learned to enjoy the rush.

If I fall over on stage? Great! That's the bit people love. They don't come to see perfection, they come to see something real.

Ricky's story is important as it shows how comparing your confidence to others can be misleading. Because what you see is often a carefully constructed illusion.

The Pros and Cons of having an alter ego

An alter ego can be like a superhero cape – useful when you need a boost. But be careful not to wear it so often that you forget who you really are underneath.

The Pros of an alter ego

- ◇ **Confidence on Demand** – Slipping into a character can make it easier to step onto a stage, deliver a presentation, or take risks you might avoid as 'yourself.'

◊ **Freedom to Experiment** – An alter ego gives you permission to push boundaries, be bolder or try out behaviours that feel uncomfortable in everyday life.

◊ **Emotional Safety Net** – If things don't go to plan, you can tell yourself, *That was the character, not me*, which reduces fear of failure.

◊ **Separation of Roles** – It can help you manage pressure by drawing a clear line between your public and private self.

The Cons of an alter ego

◊ **Detachment from Authenticity** – Relying too heavily on a persona may leave you feeling disconnected from your true self.

◊ **Exhausting to Maintain** – Keeping up a character over time can be tiring or even stressful if it doesn't match how you really feel.

◊ **Risk of Masking Deeper Issues** – An alter ego can temporarily cover nerves, but it won't address underlying confidence challenges.

◊ **Identity Confusion** – Sometimes the lines between the 'real you' and your alter ego can blur, which may feel unsettling.

So...are you tempted have a go?

EXERCISE: CREATE YOUR OWN ALTER EGO

Sometimes it is easier to step up and speak out when you have some distance from your everyday self. That's where an alter ego can help – a playful character you can 'try on' to explore different sides of your confidence.

Name Your Alter Ego

Choose a name that feels fun, bold, or powerful. (Think **Beyoncé**'s *Sasha Fierce*, **David Bowie**'s *Ziggy Stardust* or **Miley Cyrus**'s *Hannah Montana*)

Give Them Qualities

Write down three qualities your alter ego has that you would love to embody. For example, being calm, fearless, witty, commanding.

Choose a Signature Style or Symbol

Be creative! Maybe your alter ego always wears a bright scarf, stands tall with hands on hips, or sparkles in sequins and glitter?

Define Their Superpower

What does your alter ego do brilliantly that you would like to borrow? For example: She always speaks with clarity. He tells a story that grabs attention. They never worry about being judged.

Practise Stepping into Character

Next time you are preparing for a presentation, a meeting, or even just a tricky conversation, imagine slipping into your alter ego's shoes. How do they speak, move and think? Try it on for size.

TAKE FIVE: 

Flesh out more details for your alter ego. Consider what you can learn from them

Don't worry, having an alter ego doesn't make you a fake or a fraud. It is just a technique which allows you feel more comfortable in your Growth Zone.

> *Back in the day, when going on holiday with a group of my girlfriends, all in our early twenties, we each created alter egos for ourselves. For many island-hopping holidays in Greece, I was 'Mandy', and I was a hairdresser.*
>
> *I would like to take this opportunity to wholeheartedly apologise to anyone I met in Paros in 1983, who asked me for 'a quick trim'.*
>
> *I did my best!*

OK, so I'm no **Vidal Sassoon**, but sometimes it is not our practical skills which stall our progress, it is the beliefs we carry about ourselves, especially after a setback.

Client Case Study: Kelly - Rebuilding after a Career Crisis

Kelly, a creative executive, came to see me at a real career crossroads. She had left a secure role to pursue what looked like an exciting new opportunity, but quickly realised it was a mistake. In her new company she was gaslit, undermined and bullied. Resigning was the only option, but it left her unemployed and with her confidence in tatters.

Over six sessions, we worked on adjusting her core beliefs, reframing her mindset and using hypnosis to picture a future aligned with her values. Kelly also learned relaxation techniques to manage her emotions and calm her nervous system.

The transformation was remarkable. With clarity restored and her confidence rebuilt, Kelly launched her own business, which has since grown into a thriving, fulfilling career.

Kelly's story shows that even when confidence feels shattered, mindset shifts can rebuild the foundations and open doors you didn't even know were there.

 **Lauren Layfield: From Fear to Focus** 

TV and radio presenter **Lauren Layfield**, co-host of **The Dengineers** – a series which well-deserves its place in my 'Top 5 Shows I've ever Produced' list – has also learned how to reframe her mindset:

I used to think nerves meant I was going to mess up. That something was wrong. But nerves just mean it's important to you. They are a sign you care.

The first time I did live TV, my heart was beating out my chest and my hands were sweating. I thought I was going to die, or worse, get fired for being terrible!

Now, if I feel nervous, I take ten minutes to sit with it and reframe it. I tell myself that nerves just mean that it's important to me and that I want to do a good job. If that doesn't work, I give myself a bit of tough love. I pull up my 'big boy pants' and tell myself to pack it in and get a grip! I remind myself I've done this before. It's all about turning that anxious energy into focus.

Lauren also recommends everyday low-risk public speaking practice, such as chatting to your postie, saying hello to strangers, or making conversation in small moments.

"Something is only embarrassing if you are embarrassed. You have a choice."

Lauren Layfield

 ### Sam & Mark: Shared Confidence 

Sam Nixon and **Mark Rhodes** started their careers as individual contestants on *Pop Idol*, coming third and second respectively, behind the series winner, **Michelle McManus**. After a Number One hit as a singing duo, they were the perfect choice as hosts for a range of successful CBBC shows including *Top of the Pops Saturday*, *Level Up*, *Sam & Mark's Big Friday Wind Up* and the evergreen *Crackerjack*!

As a double act, they had the benefit of sharing the stage – and the nerves! However, they both agree that nerves per se, aren't bad. They are just a sign that what you're doing matters.

"It's never as nerve-wracking as you imagine it will be in your head."

Sam Nixon

"It's not rocket science! The worst that can happen is you mess up a line. No one dies."

Mark Rhodes

And on the off chance that you are considering partnering up with someone to work on a project together, their advice is to *Choose your sidekick wisely!*

"Confidence is contagious!"

Katie Thistleton

 ## Ade Adepitan MBE: The Power of Being Present

TV presenter and Paralympian **Ade Adepitan MBE** uses mindfulness to keep his nerves in check and nip the risk of 'snowballing catastrophisation' in the bud.

What exactly is Mindfulness?

Mindfulness is the practice of paying attention to the present moment with curiosity and without judgment. Instead of replaying things that happened in the past or worrying about what might happen in the future, mindfulness gently brings your awareness back to what is happening right now. It is focusing on your thoughts, feelings, body or surroundings. By noticing these experiences without trying to fight them or label them as 'good' or 'bad', you create a calmer, clearer space to respond rather than react.

> **"Be present. Enjoy the moment. Just be where you are. Being in the now is what matters."**
>
> Ade Adepitan MBE

This is great advice from Ade and the perfect introduction to another helpful exercise...

EXERCISE: QUICK AND EFFECTIVE MINDFULNESS

Five Things:

Stop and stand/sit still.

◊ Take a deep breath in through your nose and gently exhale through your mouth.

◊ Relax your neck and shoulders.

◊ Focus on and name (ideally out loud):

- Five things you can see.

- Five things you can hear.

- Five things you can feel against your skin.

Don't just guess things you might be able to see, hear or feel. For example, if you are in a familiar place, such as sitting at your desk, you could probably guess what objects you could see *without* having to look. However, it is the actual looking, listening and feeling parts which are important!

Take your time and engage all your senses. Really tune into what's happening around you, in that moment.

TAKE FIVE: 

Notice how quickly this technique calms your mind. By being fully in the present, your mind isn't dwelling on the past or worrying about the future.

> *Mindfulness is a great coping skill to whip out, whenever you need a quick mindset reset.*

 ## Michelle Ackerley: Morning Rituals and Calm Moments 

Michelle Ackerley, co-host of *Morning Live*, has built mindfulness into her early-morning routine:

*I wake up really early – my alarm is set for 4:15am – and I need quiet time. I'll put on **BBC News** or a favourite piece of music, just to protect my space. I always plan my clothes the night before, and I'm very present when doing small things like brushing my teeth, making my bed. It's almost like meditation. I try not to let my mind run away with itself and think of too many things, like what will happen if this doesn't work? I just keep pulling my mind back to the present moment.*

Interestingly, live television is when I feel the calmest, because I'm focused entirely on the now.

CONFIDENCE RULE #3:

Confidence grows when you bring your attention to the present, not to what *might* go wrong.

 **Rick Adams: Visualise for Success** 

Creative visualisation is another powerful mindset technique to stifle your nerves and quash any rising anxiety levels. It involves mentally rehearsing the thing you are about to do – vividly and in detail – so that your brain and body feel prepared.

Not convinced? Well, Emmy award-winning TV presenter, DJ and illustrator **Rick Adams** is a believer:

Creative visualisation absolutely saved my bacon!

Rick goes into more detail: *When I was anchoring a big live show on BBC1, I had loads of script to memorise and barely any rehearsal time.*

Years before, when I knocked myself out, live on television (that's another story!) I was sent to get acupuncture and to learn meditation.

And in the waiting room was a book about creative visualisation.

I started mentally rehearsing the show. Lying on my dressing room floor, eyes closed, and mentally rehearsing everything going well. It worked like magic and took all the anxiety away. It's honestly the best skill I have ever learned.

I appreciate that this might sound a bit unorthodox, but you must remember that your body responds to your thoughts, and your brain believes what it sees. Your brain doesn't know the difference between imagination and reality, it just reacts to the input. So creative visualisation is a great tool to harness this and use it to your advantage, and you will learn how to do that in Chapter 5 – Faking It.

KEY TAKEAWAY: HOW TO REFRAME YOUR MINDSET

◊ **Keep things in perspective** – nerves are normal and show you care.

◊ **Stay present** – use mindfulness to bring yourself back to the moment.

◊ **Mentally rehearse** – use creative visualisation to reduce anxiety and build confidence.

◊ **Your mindset is a tool** – and like any tool, the more you use it with intention, the stronger it becomes.

It is time to take a moment and reflect on your progress so far.

Reflection Question:

If you were to explain one insight from this chapter to a friend, what would it be and how would you describe it?

You can use your notebook or this space to jot down any helpful thoughts or reflections.

7

First Impressions

Q: Why is it important to make a good first impression?

A: There are a couple of good reasons...

One is the primacy effect: a well-established psychological principle that tells us we tend to remember the first bits of information we are given more strongly than what comes later. For example, you might be word-perfect when singing along at the start of a song you have heard before, but falter once you hit the second verse.

Another reason? Your brain is hardwired to make rapid judgments. It needs to assess, often subconsciously, whether someone is a threat. Your fight-or-flight response has a hair-trigger, so this decision-making process happens in milliseconds.

In fact, studies show that people form an impression of someone new in as little as a tenth of a second! Most impressions settle within seven to thirty seconds, and crucially, they are based mostly on visual cues.

You might think that what you say is more important than how you look, but research suggests that most communication is non-verbal. That means how you look and behave often matters more than what you say.

So, people form an impression of you based on the way you look, and that impression becomes a belief once they hear you speak.

We will look at the importance of body language in more detail in Chapter 5 – Faking It.

And there is another layer: we remember 'firsts' more vividly than routine experiences. Think of your first kiss, your first job interview or the first time you watched your favourite movie.

> *I will never forget the first time I saw **Grease** in the cinema. It was in 1978, and the queue snaked all down Queen Street in Cardiff!*
>
> *I still love that film.*

Making the Best First Impression

Understanding why first impressions matter is one thing but now let's explore how to make sure yours is a good one.

Whether you are walking into an interview, giving a presentation, attending a meeting or just introducing yourself to someone new, the goal is the same: make your presence memorable – for the right reasons!

Confidence Rule #4:

People respond more to your presence and energy than to your perfection.

Some people, like presenter **Mark Wright**, seem to do this naturally...

 **Mark Wright: Master of Natural Charm** 

Mark found fame on shows like *The Only Way Is Essex*, *I'm a Celebrity...* and *Strictly Come Dancing*, but his first foray into children's TV was co-hosting *The Dengineers* with Lauren Layfield.

Wherever the team were filming around the UK, building dream dens for some very deserving children, a small crowd would often gather on the street to watch what was going on. While this could have irritated the neighbours, Mark's presence had a disarming effect. People warmed to him instantly – even if they didn't know who he was.

People would respond positively to his warm, approachable, confident manner, and he left a good impression – not just of himself but of the whole production team. Result!

> *I know that Mark enjoyed the experience of filming The Dengineers much more than he did on the other series we made together: **Workout the Wright Way.***
>
> *That one was made under the tightest lockdown restrictions, which meant that Mark had to film six weeks' worth of daily exercise shows in his home gym, by himself. The Production team wasn't allowed on site, so we directed everything over Zoom.*
>
> *Remarkably, we are still friends!*

Q: I'm not Mark Wright, so how can I increase my chances of creating a great first impression?

A: Great question! Let's break this down into three-pronged approach:

- ◊ *What (or not) to wear*

- ◊ *How to behave*

- ◊ *What to say*

1. What (or not) to wear

Your clothes are a powerful part of the first impression puzzle – especially in those crucial first thirty seconds, before you have spoken a word.

Dress appropriately for the context/occasion but always stay true to yourself. Look like you, because comfort breeds confidence.

"Make sure you are comfortable in what you're wearing. The last thing you want is to be worrying: Is my dress too short? Have I got the right tie on? Am I going to fall over in these heels? That way, you can concentrate fully on what you are doing."

Lauren Layfield

It goes without saying that whatever you wear, you should look clean and presentable. Do some online research and check out the company's website and/or social channels to see how other people dress at work, what they wear to social occasions, networking events, etc. See how you can match their tone without mimicking.

I have lost count of the number of people who arrived wearing a smart suit for their first day on a BBC work placement...only to come back the following day, dressed much more casually.

Authenticity matters. If people have already seen you on social media, you don't want to show up looking like someone else dressed you.

However, it's worth noting that TV presenters regularly work with stylists to achieve a specific look, so technically some are being dressed by someone else.

Many shops now offer a personal shopper/stylist service, so getting professional help with your outfit is not exclusively for celebrities. There are also plenty of online stylists offering their fashion advice and expertise for free.

"Work out what your magical and unique qualities are."

Sally Gray MBE

I am stressing the importance of getting your 'look' right as I, unfortunately, have first-hand experience of getting this very, very wrong! Even now, almost four decades later, I still cringe at the memory.

My Case Study: A Lesson from the 80s

In 1987, I was working at **Wales Today** in BBC Cardiff and spotted an advert for a brand-new series which was crewing up in London. I sent off my CV and a VHS(!) of a film I had made - and I was thrilled to be shortlisted and invited for an interview.

(If you've never heard of a VHS, it was a precursor to the DVD.)

Unfortunately, the internet (as we now know it) didn't exist in 1987, so I couldn't research any information online. So, I did the next best thing...I followed my mum's advice!

I rocked up to my interview wearing my older sister's (Karen) Paul Costello, Air Force blue cashmere skirt suit and a cream roll-neck jumper. It was the 1980s, so massive shoulder pads were de rigueur! I looked polished...but I didn't feel like me.

I walked in feeling confident – until I met the interviewers: **Janet Street-Porter** and **Jane Hewland**. I didn't know at the time, but the show would later become **Network 7**, the pioneer of the rebellious 'Yoof TV' movement.

So, picture me in a conservative skirt suit, sitting across from two creative powerhouses with neon hair, punky prints and unapologetic attitudes. I looked out of place, and more importantly, I felt out of place.

> *It felt like I'd been shoved on stage in the wrong costume, without knowing any of the lines!*

I could feel all my youthful confidence and misplaced optimism drain from my body. I completely clammed up. My mind went blank. Time stood still and I couldn't wait to get out of there. It was a humiliating and humbling experience.

Unsurprisingly, I didn't get the job.

However, that interview-from-hell taught me an important life lesson, and I vowed to never make that mistake again. From that day forward, I always showed up as myself, not a version of what I *thought* someone wanted me to be.

Sometimes I got the job, sometimes I didn't, but I always left the interview knowing they had met the real Annette Williams.

Despite working in the same industry, I didn't cross paths with Janet again for another 26 years.

But when I did (at Les Dennis's 60th birthday party), I told her the story of how that humiliating experience had been a real turning point for me.

Interestingly, Janet had no recollection of the incident, which I had been replaying in my mind for well over two decades!

Wear something that makes you feel like the best version of yourself. Confidence can't thrive when you are in someone else's shoes…or your sister's suit!

"You can't control what others think – you just have to do you."

Angellica Bell

2. How to Behave

During that 1987 interview, I made a rookie mistake: I turned my attention inward. I couldn't recall the details of anything they had asked me, because I was completely inside my own head.

I focused entirely on how anxious I felt, not on the people in front of me, the room I was in or the opportunity. My internal spotlight became a trap.

When I work with clients experiencing social anxiety, performance nerves or glossophobia (fear of public speaking), we work on shifting their attention outward. Because if you concentrate on what is happening externally, rather than internally, you can reduce your anxiety levels.

This is a simple but very effective technique and works well with or without hypnosis

EXERCISE: SHIFT YOUR FOCUS OF ATTENTION

Next time you feel anxiety rising:

◊ Take a deep breath in through your nose and exhale gently through your mouth. Then continue to breathe in a gentle rhythm.

◊ Notice something or someone you can see, close by.

◊ Examine it/them. Notice colours, textures, shapes, patterns. Really look closely at that object or person.

◊ What else do you notice?

◊ Now shift your focus in another direction. What are you looking at now?

◊ Take time to study all the details

◊ Every time you become aware of your thoughts drifting inwards, gently return your attention back to what you can see.

This isn't just distraction, it is a proven grounding technique that helps calm the nervous system.

It's Not About You!

As a TV producer, I would often have to remind presenters – and myself – of this core truth: *It is not about you. It's about the audience.*

Your performance, your message, your story exists to serve and benefit others. The more you focus on what the audience needs from you, the less power anxiety has over you.

As a kids' TV producer, I certainly wasn't in the target demographic of six to twelve, so I learned to step into my audience's shoes because...**It's Not About You!**

 ## Angela Lamont: Audience First 

Presenter and Emcee Angela regularly hosts events for large, live audiences. So how does she make a confident impression and engage an audience of thousands of people?

I find out who they are, what they care about, and then give them something useful. No one minds listening if they learn something that makes life easier, saves them time or saves money.

 ## Angellica Bell: Respect the Audience 

For Angellica, being respectful and honest with her audience is non-negotiable – even if it pushes her out of her Comfort Zone.

She recalls one unexpectedly emotional moment during a radio interview with presenter **Fleur East**. They were talking about the importance of positive Black role models on national TV and how Angellica's presence on CBBC had influenced a generation of children — including Fleur herself.

I felt so overwhelmed. I'm not a crier, but I couldn't hide my true feelings. I always try to be respectful and honest, and in that moment I couldn't – and didn't want to – hide what I was feeling. If I'd tried to, the audience would have known.

That raw honesty is the essence of authentic confidence – the courage to stay connected, even when emotion takes you by surprise.

Tips to remember:

⋄   Get out of your head and into the room.

⋄   Make eye contact. Smile. Look friendly.

⋄   Stay focused on the people you are talking to.

⋄   It's Not About You!

3. What to say

We will go into more detail about vocal delivery in the next chapter – The Voice – but first, let's talk 'structure'.

Most of the professionals I interviewed agreed that you should avoid starting any type of important conversation or presentation without having a rough structure or plan of what you are going to say.

Don't wing it. Even if you are confident, go in with a plan.

"Keep it natural. Use bullet points to outline a clear start, middle and end. But keep it flexible so you can bring it to life in your own way."

Mark Wright

"If I nail the intro, I feel happy. Rehearse it so it becomes muscle memory. And if nerves hit? Drop any tricky words to make it easier for you. Don't booby trap yourself!"

Sally Gray MBE

"Think of your talk like the shape of a capital W - not an M.[1]"

Ted Robbins (based on his dad's advice to **The Beatles**)

1. According to Sir Paul McCartney in his biography *Many Years from Now*, The Beatles used the W format for all their live performances.

The W Format:

◊ Start high with a strong, engaging opening

◊ Slight dip, as you ease into the core content

◊ Mid-lift to raise the energy again

◊ Dip again to relax and reset

◊ End on a high and finish with impact

Remember the W: Memorable. Dynamic. Balanced.

KEY TAKEAWAYS

◊ First impressions happen fast – usually before you speak.

◊ What you wear matters. Be clean, context-appropriate and true to yourself.

◊ Shift attention outward to reduce nerves.

◊ Focus on what your audience needs. It's NOT about you!

◊ Structure your message. Start strong. End stronger

OK, it is time to pause and reflect.

When you meet someone new, what do you think they notice about you first – and what would you like them to notice?

You can use your notebook or this space to jot down any helpful thoughts or reflections.

IMPORTANT: Preparation for the next chapter

Before we go any further, it is time to assess your current communication skills. Remember: Confidence is not something you are born with. It is a skill, and it gets stronger with practice.

EXERCISE: RECORD YOURSELF ON CAMERA

1. You are going to record yourself speaking for five minutes.

2. Choose any topic you enjoy, are passionate or knowledgeable about, e.g. food, sport, your family, favourite holiday destination, dog grooming tips, reality TV...whatever!

3. Ideally stand up (or sit up tall) and look directly at the camera lens on your phone or laptop.

   TIP: Find somewhere private to do this if you don't feel audience-ready yet!

4. Take a calming breath, relax and smile.

5. Set a timer for five minutes, press Record and start talking. Just let the words flow and don't stop until the timer ends.

This recording is just for you. Now watch it back – multiple times. Notice how you speak, how you stand, how you come across. What feels good? What could be better?

You can make notes below or in your journal.

Grab your camera and give it a go. Your future self will thank you.

Observations from your 5-minute video recording:

How easy was it to keep talking for 5 minutes? Did what you say make sense?

What do you notice about your body language? Any unusual behaviours or mannerisms?

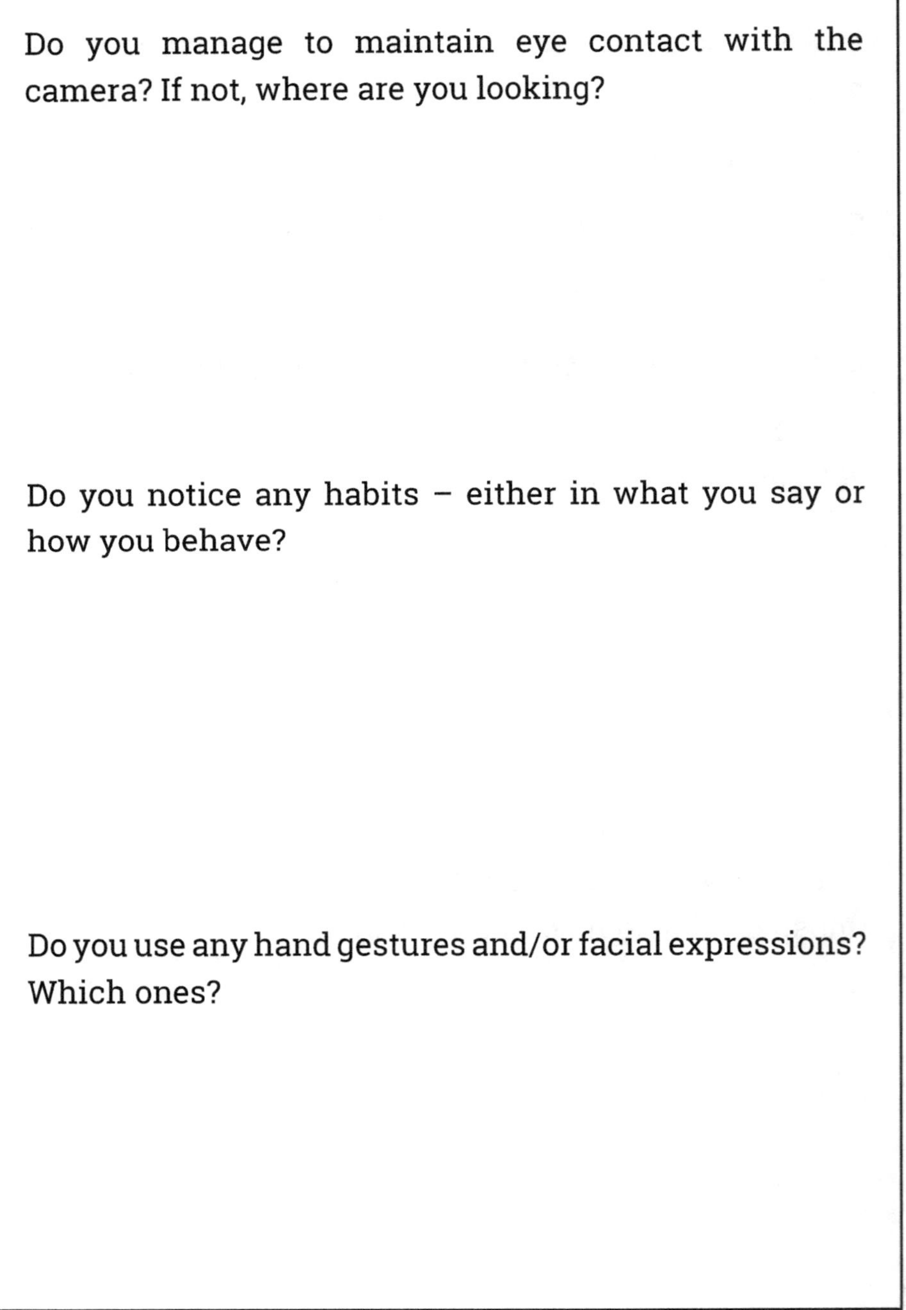
Do you manage to maintain eye contact with the camera? If not, where are you looking?

Do you notice any habits – either in what you say or how you behave?

Do you use any hand gestures and/or facial expressions? Which ones?

When speaking, do you use any 'filler words', e.g. *um, sort of, you know, like, well, so*?

On a confidence scale of 1 – 10 (10 = maximum), how would rate your performance? Be honest!

What positive points do you notice? (There <u>will</u> be some!)

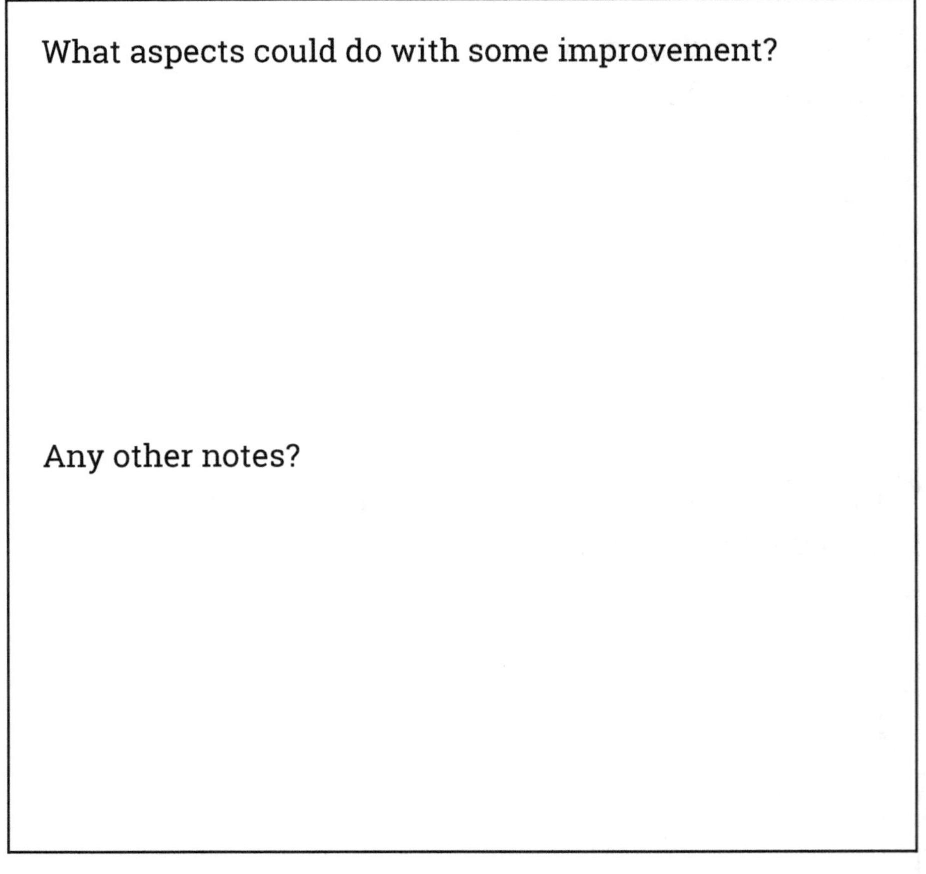

Please keep this recording. It will be helpful to refer to it as you progress through the rest of the exercises in this book. And I recommend that you repeat this exercise once you have completed the whole process.

You will be able to see for yourself how much you have improved by comparing the two recordings.

6

The Voice

If I had a pound every time someone said to me: *I don't like the sound of my voice*, I would be writing this book from the balcony of my waterfront property in Mallorca!

I exaggerate to make a point. I would probably be in Anglesey!

Most people dislike hearing their voice played back because it sounds different from what they hear in their own head. There is a scientific explanation for this phenomenon: voice confrontation.

When we speak, we hear our voice internally through bone conduction (vibrations in the skull) as well as externally via air conduction. Bone conduction adds resonance, giving our voice a richer, deeper quality. But when others hear us – or when we hear a recording – it is only through air conduction. The result is a thinner, unfamiliar sound that clashes with what we expect.

Q: So how can you learn to love your voice?

A: By appreciating the glorious range of everything it can do!

Imagine your voice as a piano keyboard. You have got access to the full 88 keys, but most people limit themselves to playing 'Chopsticks'. Meanwhile, confident speakers are playing **Mozart** and improvising jazz!

If you want to develop vocal mastery, you need to practise and step out of your Comfort Zone into your Growth Zone.

Even concert pianists start by practising scales!

(I am slightly worried I might have overplayed the music metaphor, but I hope you understand what I mean.)

When you are nervous, one of the first places it shows is in your voice. The fight-or-flight response tenses the muscles in your neck and jaw, shortens your breathing and tightens your vocal cords, making your voice sound strained or weak.

So that's why, when you finally find the courage to speak up in a meeting, your voice might come out more like a strangled whimper than the confident tone you had hoped for.

But there is some good news...

Confidence Rule #5:

Your voice is a tool. The more you use it, the stronger and more confident it becomes.

In this chapter, we will explore three key aspects:

◊ Volume

◊ Pitch, Melody and Tone

◊ The Power of the Pause

(A quick heads-up: In the next chapter, we will bring this together with non-verbal skills to help you exude full-body confidence!)

TAKE FIVE:

Whose voice do you love listening to and are there any which grate on you? Try and identify what it is about those voices that you like/dislike? Think about any voices which make you feel something, whenever you hear them.

 ## Jamie Theakston: Value Your Voice 

For any presenter, your voice is your trademark. So, imagine the fear TV and radio presenter **Jamie Theakston** must have felt when he received news that his livelihood – and potentially his life – were at risk when he was diagnosed with laryngeal cancer in 2024.

I worked with Jamie on *Live & Kicking*, where he was 50% of a brilliant TV couple, alongside **Zoe Ball**. Since 2005, Jamie's voice has been a welcome presence on the airwaves, as co-host of *Heart Breakfast* on *Heart Radio*.

The earliest signs of his illness were subtle. Jamie thought he just had a sore throat. However, listeners noticed a change in the warm, distinctive tone of his voice and contacted the radio station. That outside observation saved his life.

Jamie was diagnosed with stage 1 laryngeal cancer, a rare disease often detected through voice changes.

On **Davina McCall's** *Begin Again* podcast, Jamie explains that he underwent three separate operations on his vocal cords and acknowledges that he came *dangerously close to not being able to speak.*

Thanks to early diagnosis, Jamie has recovered and is back on air. His voice, though still not back to its former full range, is regaining strength through daily vocal exercises.

It's still weak, but it's getting stronger every day.

Jamie's story is a powerful reminder of how precious and trainable your voice is.

Volume

Imagine your vocal volume on a scale from zero (silent) to ten (shouting). Where are you most comfortable? When you listened back to your five-minute recording (Chapter 7), what level were you speaking at?

Most people with low confidence speak at a level four or perhaps a five. But if you want to sound confident, aim for a seven.

Try this: Go somewhere you're not known and respond to everyday questions at a seven-level volume. No one knows who you are, so they won't notice any difference.

Q: Do you want fries with that?

A: YES PLEASE!

It will feel strange at first, but your vocal cords will get used to it. And the more you practise, the more natural it becomes.

Once you are comfortable at a confident seven, you can play with volume for effect. Don't stay at the same level throughout your conversation or presentation. Just dial it up or down, depending on what you want to emphasise.

Pro Tip: Always match your volume to your space. Big room = big voice. Small space = quieter voice.

Example: Hospital bedside = four or five. Telling people to flee a burning building = Ten!

Online meeting = aim for a level six or seven.

 **Lauren Layfield: Voice and Vulnerability** 

Radio is incredibly intimate, in a way that TV often isn't. There is no visual distraction, so it's just your voice and your listener. I often trip over my words and worry it sounds terrible, but when I listen back, I realise it's totally fine. I didn't sound awful. I sound human, not a robot.

Pitch, Melody and Tone

Pitch, melody and tone help make what you say more memorable and engaging. In turn, this adds to your confidence aura.

Monotone voices are dull and forgettable. Monotone information being delivered at you is easily forgettable.

Confident people vary the rhythm and energy of their voice. Think of it as singing your speech (just less musical). As Lauren said, *we're not robots,* so you need to make sure you add more expression to what you are saying.

Techniques to try:

◊ Vary your rhythm and melody throughout.

◊ Slow down for emphasis.

◊ Drop your pitch at the end of statements – it sounds more confident. An upward end sounds like a half-formed question.

◊ Use facial expressions and body language to energise your voice.

◊ Expressionless face + monotone delivery = BORING.

 **Jez Edwards: Vocal Preparation** 

Jez and I have worked on several different series together, including **Xchange** and **Record Breakers**.

Despite having been a presenter, voiceover artist and actor for decades, Jez always goes back to basics when preparing for any new role: *Repetition is key. I start with straight reads, then build up energy and delivery. If the script requires movement, I learn it moving. I break it into a beginning, middle and end – like telling a story. That flow gives me confidence.*

The Power of the Pause

NEVER underestimate the power of the Pause!

When nerves kick in, your brain screams: *Get this over with – FAST!* So, you rush.

But speed undermines confidence. Pausing, on the other hand, shows authority.

"Nerves make me speed up, so I always deliver my opening line twice as slowly. Once I've started clearly and confidently, I feel in control. It's like throwing down an anchor – once that's done, you steady the ship."

Angellica Bell

Why Pauses Work:

◊ They give your audience time to absorb your words.

◊ They give you time to breathe and stay grounded.

◊ They reduce the likelihood of filler words such as *um, like*, and *you know*.

◊ They invite interaction and can create drama.

"I never rush. My rhythm is guided by the audience's feedback. That first response or ripple of laughter tells me I'm on the right track and calms me."

Ortis Deley

> **Learn to love the pause.**

Client Case Study: Lara – Rediscovering Her Voice

You might imagine that business coaches brim with confidence when it comes to speaking, but even seasoned professionals can find themselves gripped by fear.

Lara, a business coach in the United States, had developed a growing fear of public speaking in the years after COVID. There was no single trigger; the anxiety had simply crept up until she found herself turning down opportunities that could have elevated her career.

Despite the thousands of miles between us, we worked together virtually to challenge her beliefs and reframe her mindset. I also drew on my TV production experience to share practical presenting techniques, while hypnosis and calming strategies gave her a sense of inner steadiness.

Soon after, Lara was back on stage – not only speaking with confidence but enjoying it.

Her story is proof that confidence coaching and hypnotherapy can transcend geography. The tools work wherever you are in the world

It's Practice Time!

Here's a fun vocal warm-up I often use with hypnotherapy clients who fear public speaking. It is a great way to gently ease them into using their voice in a more engaging and confident way. You have probably done this instinctively if you have ever read a bedtime story to a child.

EXERCISE: READ IT LIKE YOU MEAN IT!

Read a short children's story aloud with full expression.

◊   Experiment with pitch, volume, pace and tone.

◊   Try using character voices or dramatic pauses.

◊   Be playful.

◊   Read it to a child, a pet, or even your sofa cushions.

The goal? Get comfortable using your full vocal range.

Don't have a children's book to hand? No problem... *Here's one I made earlier!*

Suggested character voices:

Muffin the cavapoochon: Soft, breathy, a little anxious – like she's always on the edge of a sneeze.

Crumpet the hamster: Fast, high and bossy – the tone of someone who's absolutely in charge (but very small).

Cariad the dragon: Deep, warm, a bit unsure – imagine a friendly Welsh dragon who hasn't realised she's a dragon!

Challenge yourself:

◊ Try reading with exaggerated emotion.

◊ Repeat a line three different ways.

◊ Change the story's pace.

◊ Make yourself laugh.

Muffin, Crumpet
and the
Dragon Who Didn't
Know

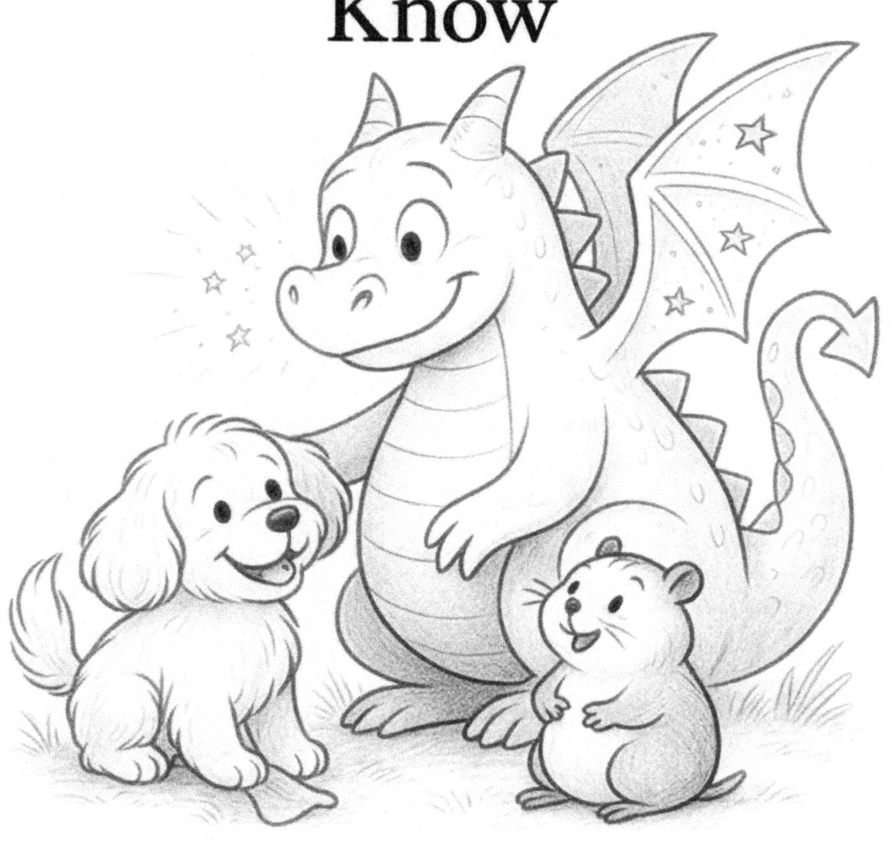

A read-aloud story for grown-ups who are ready
to discover the joy of using their voice

One sunny morning, Muffin the cavapoochon was in the garden, nibbling on her comfort blanket.

"Oh crumbs," she whispered. **"What if today's the day everything goes terribly, terribly wrong?"**

Crumpet the hamster popped out of a flowerpot, paws on hips. **"Muffin!"** he squeaked. **"For the last time, the clouds are NOT made of mashed potatoes, and they are NOT going to fall on your head."**

"But they could," Muffin muttered. **"What if they are heavy mash?"**

Just then, a great **WHOOOSH** swept through the garden.

"HULLOOOO!" It was Cariad the dragon, landing with a flurry of glittery wings and a crash into the compost heap.

Muffin shrieked. Crumpet fell over. Cariad blinked.

"What's the matter? Was it something I said?"

"Cariad," Muffin said, trying to sound braver than she felt, **"You're just a little…big."**

"And you don't always look where you're going," added Crumpet, brushing compost off his bottom.

"I'm sorry?" gasped Cariad. **"Did I land on anyone's sandwiches?"**

Crumpet crossed his tiny arms. **"No. But you made a right mess of the compost heap."**

"**Oh no! I'm sorry.**" said Cariad. "**I was just excited to get here and see my two fluffy best friends.**"

"**Oh Cariad. You are a funny dragon,**" Muffin whispered with a smile.

"**You just have to remember that you're not like us,**" added Crumpet.

Cariad looked down at her huge claws. She wiggled her tail. She puffed out a little sparkle sneeze. **"I suppose I'm not like anyone,"** she said softly.

Crumpet kicked a pebble. **"Yes. You're not like anyone else. But that's what makes you brilliant."**

Cariad sniffled. Her voice wobbled like jelly. **"Do you really think so? Even with my clompy feet and sneezy sparkles?"**

Muffin gave her a lick on the snout. **"We're all a bit different. I panic about mashed potato clouds. Crumpet yells at butterflies."**

"THEY STARTED IT!" shouted Crumpet from inside a welly boot.

They all laughed. Cariad gave them a dragon-sized cuddle. **"So, what now?"** she said, perking up.

Crumpet rubbed his paws together. **"I think we should find out what dragons are REALLY good at. Come on, it's Adventure Time!"**

"Can I bring my blanket?" said Muffin.

"I've got extra marshmallows!" said Cariad.

"And not forgetting my emergency peanut!?" said Crumpet.

And off they went. A fluffy worrier, a pint-sized bossy-boots, and a sparkly dragon who still didn't quite know what made her special.

But she was about to find out.

TO BE CONTINUED...

TAKE FIVE:

How did you find that exercise? Borrow other children's books and keep experimenting with different voices. Notice how much more energy and impact the stories have.

If you have or know any small children, I'm sure they would love to have some extra story time with you!

KEY TAKEAWAYS:

◊ Most people dislike their voice because of **voice confrontation** – it sounds different when recorded.

◊ **Your voice is like a piano** – full of potential. Use all the keys.

◊ **Volume:** Practise speaking at level seven to sound more confident.

◊ **Pitch, melody and tone:** Vary your delivery for interest and impact.

◊ **Pauses:** Give your audience (and yourself) breathing space.

◊ **Confidence in your voice** comes from practice, not perfection.

The Voice has been a fact-filled chapter and there is a lot of information to digest.

Pause and reflect on what you have learned. Jot down your thoughts on this page or in your journal.

Reflection Question:

When do you feel most confident using your voice, and how could you create more of those moments in everyday life?

When you're ready, let's move on...

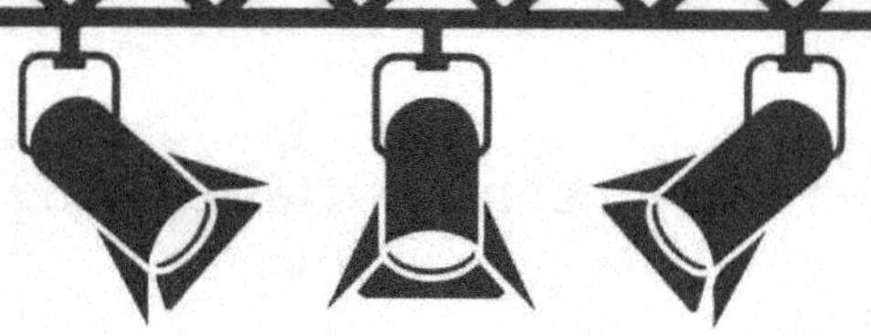

5

Faking It

I am aware that this might be a controversial title, because advice like *Fake it 'til you make it* or *Be it to believe it* is often dished out as the antidote to Imposter Syndrome. And while it is well-intentioned, it can sound like a contradiction when we are also told to be our authentic selves.

It's all very confusing!

But these aren't just slogans you might see printed on a T-shirt. The idea of 'acting as if' is rooted in well-established principles from cognitive behavioural therapy (CBT) and behaviour therapy, particularly the work of psychologist Andrew Salter, one of the early pioneers of assertiveness training.

A Quick Note on Imposter Syndrome

Imposter Syndrome is the persistent belief that you are not as capable, competent or successful as others think you are, and that it is only a matter of time before you are 'found out'.

Even when there is plenty of evidence that you are doing a great job, you might still feel like a fraud and that you have somehow tricked everyone into overestimating your abilities.

It often sounds like:

- ◊ *I'm not really qualified to be here.*

- ◊ *They are going to realise I have no idea what I'm doing.*

- ◊ *I just got lucky – I don't actually deserve this.*

It is surprisingly common, especially among high-achievers and perfectionists, and even more so for women in competitive or male-dominated environments. While not a clinical diagnosis, Imposter Syndrome can have a real impact on confidence and career progression.

But here is the good news: Imposter Syndrome doesn't mean something is wrong with you. It means you have internalised a belief that needs rebalancing – and that starts with changing what you do.

That is where 'Acting As If' comes in...

Salter's theory suggests that, if you want to feel different, start by *acting* different. In other words, behaviour isn't just a result of how we feel, it also *shapes* how we feel.

Acting Your Way into Confidence

In CBT, we understand that thoughts, feelings and behaviours are part of a feedback loop. Traditionally, we think it works like this:

I feel confident → *so I act confident* → *which reinforces my belief that I am confident.*

But Salter flipped that idea on its head and asked:

What if you acted confident first, even if you didn't feel it? Would your mind catch up?

Spoiler Alert: Yes, it usually does.

That is because your brain is constantly interpreting what your body is doing. If you stand tall, smile, hold eye contact, speak clearly and take up space, your brain starts receiving signals that say: *Oh, we must be feeling confident!*

This isn't self-deception. It is self-direction. You are choosing to send your mind down a more helpful path.

In cognitive behavioural hypnotherapy, I use this technique to help clients build their social confidence, reduce anxiety, or overcome Imposter Syndrome.

In hypnosis, they get to rehearse this new behaviour in the safety of the therapy room first.

By encouraging people to act in ways that match the version of themselves they want to become, we are helping rewire their internal experience to align with that behaviour.

It's not about faking – It's about rehearsal

Let's get one thing clear, 'acting as if' is not being fake or dishonest. It is not about putting on a mask or pretending to be someone you're not.

It is about rehearsing the version of you that already exists but perhaps hasn't had much stage time yet.

You are not making it up. You are bringing it out.

In the same way an actor prepares for a role – by practising lines, gestures, tone of voice – you are practising confidence behaviours. And through that practice, you begin to *feel* more confident too.

Remember when Ricky Wilson went to art college, he suddenly stared to act 'as if' he was confident – and the seed for *Kaiser Chief's* frontman, 'Ricky', was sewn!

Q: *What would a 'confident you' look and behave like?*

A: *Well, there is only one way to find out!*

**EXERCISE: REHEARSING THE ROLE
– CREATIVE VISUALISATION**

Let's borrow from both cognitive behavioural therapy and the acting world here. You are going to treat confidence like a character – one that you are going to rehearse, step into, and eventually embody.

Close your eyes and start by imagining a version of yourself who already has the confidence you're aiming for. You at your best. Maybe they are calm and self-assured when they walk into a meeting. Maybe they speak with ease in front of a group. Maybe they walk tall, make eye contact, and don't apologise for taking up space.

> *Don't forget! This is how Paul McKenna helped Les Dennis overcome his press night nerves.*
>
> My tip to super-charge your imagination is to engage all your senses. What can you see, hear, smell, touch, etc.? Imagine being in that situation, in real time, rather than watching yourself in that situation, from a distance.

However, be aware that approximately 1%–4% of the population cannot imagine visually. This is called aphantasia. But don't worry if this is you, because you can still practise creative visualisation.

What is Aphantasia?

Aphantasia is the inability to create mental pictures in your mind's eye. While many people can close their eyes and 'see' an image (like a beach or a friend's face), those with aphantasia don't experience this kind of visual imagination. Instead, their minds may stay blank when asked to picture something.

Other Ways to Imagine

Even without mental pictures, people with aphantasia often have rich imaginations – they just use them differently. For example, they may:

◊ **Think in words** – describing scenes or ideas in detail as an internal narrative.

- **Use sounds** – recalling voices, music or environmental noises to bring ideas to life.

- **Rely on feelings** – focusing on the emotions or physical sensations linked to a memory or idea.

- **Draw on logic or facts** – building a scene by reasoning through what must be there.

- **Express externally** – sketching, writing or physically acting things out to explore ideas.

In short: imagination isn't limited to pictures – it can be verbal, emotional, sensory or physical. People with aphantasia often excel by leaning on these other strengths.

EXERCISE: 'ACT AS IF' – A CONFIDENCE REHEARSAL

Step 1: Choose Your Situation

Pick a real scenario where you want to feel more confident. It could be an upcoming presentation, a networking event, a difficult conversation, or even entering a room full of people.

Remember everything you have learned so far about verbal and non-verbal communication.

Step 2: Learn the Role

Close your eyes and activate your imagination.

Ask yourself:

◊   How would a confident version of me enter this room or situation? Feel it.

◊   What would I be wearing? See it.

◊   How would I sit or stand? Do it.

◊   What kind of facial expression would I have? Try it.

◊   How would I greet people? Practise it.

◊   What kind of language would they use? Say it.

You can even draw inspiration from confident people you admire: TV presenters, charismatic leaders or even someone you know in real life. This isn't imitation, it is inspiration.

Step 3: Step Into the Role

◊   Now practise: at home in front of a mirror, on your phone camera, out on a solo walk – wherever you have the opportunity.

◊   Stand or sit as the 'new you' would.

◊   Speak a few lines aloud, using your new posture and tone.

◊   Notice what changes in your energy, your voice, even your breathing.

> **Step 4: Do it for real!**
>
> Next time you are in a confidence-challenging moment, remind yourself: *I don't have to wait to feel confident to act confident. I can act as if, and the feelings will follow.*
>
> You are not faking it. You are training your brain and body to work together and sending the signal that **Confidence Lives Here**.

> *Now, **Confidence Lives Here** would look good on a T-Shirt!*

A Word of Reassurance

You might feel silly doing this at first – that is totally normal.

But remember, this is exactly how professional performers prepare. They rehearse. They warm up. They step into the version of themselves required for the moment. Confidence isn't a trait they were born with, it is a role they have practised into muscle memory.

And with repetition, it starts to feel real – because it *is* real.

Confidence Rule #6:

Confidence grows from action. Sometimes you need to act 'as if' until your feelings catch up.

TAKE FIVE:

How did you feel during the **creative visualisation** exercise? Were any of your senses more powerful or vivid than the others?

Had you been aware of this difference before you tried the exercise? Knowing your dominant senses will make visualisation more impactful.

 **Rick Adams: Be Bold, Be You** 

TV presenter **Rick Adams**, known for his brilliantly cheeky humour on both sides of the Atlantic, took 'acting as if' to a whole new level when he accepted his Emmy award via video link: *I wanted to show up in a way that felt like me, so I accepted the award sat semi-naked, wearing just a bow tie, in a room that looked like a sauna! I just relaxed and went for it. I loved every moment.*

Rick's story is a perfect reminder that 'acting as if' doesn't mean playing it safe, it means showing up fully and authentically.

And no, 'acting as if' is not just for TV types. Anyone can do this.

Client Case Study: Dawn

Dawn is an accomplished and knowledgeable expert. She is regularly invited to speak at global conferences and gets frequent requests for TV and radio interviews.

But behind the scenes, Dawn used to dread live presentations, and her anxiety would spiral in the lead-up to each one, every time.

I saw Dawn for three sessions, as that was all the time she had before her next big talk. We worked through the steps you have just read about in the previous chapters: grounding, visualisation, rehearsal.

Her biggest hurdle wasn't understanding the techniques. It was applying them under pressure. Through guided hypnosis, we rehearsed her 'confident self' in a calm, focused state.

Once Dawn experienced what it *felt like* to act confident, it didn't seem so out of reach anymore.

A few days later, Dawn delivered her best presentation yet.

Believe me, 'acting as if' works!

Katie Thistleton: Don't Stress Over Mistakes

Katie is now a well-known author, TV presenter and a familiar voice on **Radio 1**, but her TV career started working in the production offices at CBeebies and CBBC, rather than in front of the camera. So, Katie also had the perfect vantage point to observe confidence in action, before she stepped into her spotlight, and she admits that 'faking it' became her turning point:

I do this every day in my job! I had an epiphany that if you fake that you're confident and unphased by things, you actually end up feeling that way. It wasn't until then that I became really good at my job. I realised the best presenters aren't the ones who never make mistakes, they're the ones who can confidently make them, laugh them off and move on.

Early in her career, Katie says she tried to appear *cool enough* and hid behind a polished façade. Now she embraces mistakes, calls them out, and even laughs at them on air.

I literally don't care anymore. Years of live TV and radio have taught me that being unapologetically yourself is the ultimate confidence.

Katie's story is a brilliant reminder that faking confidence isn't about pretending to be someone else; it's about allowing the confident version of you to finally step forward.

KEY TAKEAWAYS: FAKING IT – THE SCIENCE BEHIND 'ACTING AS IF'

◊ *Fake it 'til you make it* isn't about being inauthentic – it is rooted in behavioural science.

◊ Imposter Syndrome is a common internal voice that says *I'm not good enough* – even when all the evidence says otherwise.

◊ According to psychologist Andrew Salter, behaviour can lead emotion, so acting confident can help you feel confident.

◊ Your brain takes cues from your body. When you stand, speak and move like a confident person, your thoughts start to shift too.

◊ 'Acting as if' is a way of rehearsing the version of you that already exists, not pretending to be someone you're not.

◊ Even professional presenters rehearse confidence – it's not fake, it's training.

◊ You don't have to wait to feel ready. Start behaving like the person you want to become and let your feelings catch up.

Good news – you are now well past the halfway mark. Take a moment to reflect on how far you have come and the progress you have made. Note any changes to how you are feeling and behaving. It feels good, doesn't it?

Reflection Question:

If you were to borrow the confidence of a movie character, rock star or superhero for a day, who would it be – and how would you show up differently?

Use this space or your journal to jot down any helpful thoughts or reflections.

4

It'll be Alright on the Night

If you have watched British TV at any point from the late 1970s to the current day, you will probably be aware of the TV 'bloopers' show ***It'll be Alright on the Night***.

This ubiquitous series celebrates the unplanned things that can sometimes go wrong on screen...and I'm not ashamed to admit that clips from some of my shows have been featured for millions of viewers to laugh at!

Ironically, the title and content of the show is contrary to the *It'll be alright on the night* phrase's intended use. Because the original purpose was to reassure theatre performers that even if rehearsals go badly, the live performance will be OK.

However, for the purposes of this chapter, please consider *It'll be alright on the night* as a mindset prompt – a calm, grounded belief that things will work out.

Because here is the truth: the best way to reduce anxiety is to increase relaxation. Once you are more relaxed, your thoughts become clearer, your heart rate slows, and you are less likely to be hijacked by nerves.

Confidence Rule #7:

Remember: It is physically impossible to be anxious and relaxed at the same time!

If you need further reassurance, let's take a quick look at the psychological theory that explains how this works.

Understanding Anxiety and Confidence: Beck's Formula

You might be surprised to hear that confidence – or a lack of it – can be explained almost mathematically.

According to psychologist and CBT pioneer **Dr. Aaron T. Beck**, anxiety arises when we overestimate the threat of a situation and underestimate our ability to cope with it.

Beck's theory proposes that our emotional response (like anxiety, fear or hesitation) is shaped by the balance between two key factors:

1. How bad you think the outcome will be, and

2. How well you think you will be able to handle it

Or, as expressed as a simple formula:

$$\text{Anxiety} = \frac{\text{Probability} \times \text{Awfulness}}{\text{Ability to Cope}}$$

Let's break that equation down…

Probability: How likely you think something bad is going to happen.

Awfulness: How terrible you think it would be if it did happen.

Ability to Cope: How well you believe you could handle it, practically and emotionally.

So, if your inner voice is saying: *I'm definitely going to mess this up* (high probability), *it'll be humiliating* (maximum awfulness), and *I won't be able to cope* (low ability) …

…then your anxiety levels *will* spike.

But if you tweak any part of that equation, even slightly – by lowering the probability, softening the outcome or increasing your belief in your ability to cope – your anxiety reduces, and your confidence rises.

The Confidence Equation

This theory also explains the key difference between someone who feels confident and someone who doesn't.

It is not always about skill or experience. Often, the only real difference is in how strongly someone believes they can handle it, whatever 'it' is.

Confidence = I can cope with 'it'

Anxiety = I can't cope with 'it'

It is as simple and as powerful as that!

So, if you want to boost your confidence, one of the most effective ways to do it is by increasing your perceived ability to cope.

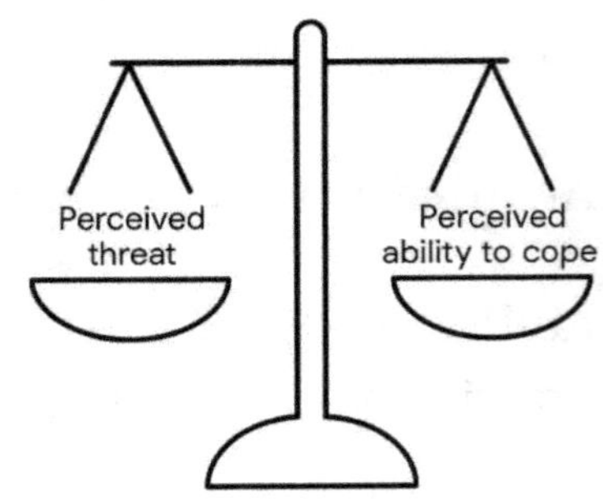

I have said it before, but it is worth repeating...the best way to reduce anxiety is by increasing relaxation.

And this is why you need to adopt the mindset: *It'll be Alright on the Night!*

Client Case Study: Mary – When imagination fuels fear

A vivid imagination can be a gift – but when it turns against you, it fuels fears that feel impossible to challenge.

Mary had avoided essential dental work for years due to an intense fear of the dentist. Her creative mind would conjure endless horrific scenarios, each one more terrifying than the last.

Together, we identified the root of her fear: catastrophisation. Once Mary realised her imagination was creating these fears – and that if you can create them, you can also change them – the shift was immediate.

I helped Mary learn how to relax on demand by using her vivid imagination to whisk herself away to somewhere she felt safe, happy and completely relaxed – her back garden.

So, Mary was blissfully unaware of what the dentist was doing in her mouth, because in her imagination, she was relaxing in her back garden. Just pottering around and quietly admiring all her beautiful flowers, hearing the birdsong and feeling a gentle warm breeze on her skin.

Her body remained relaxed throughout the procedure. Mary still doesn't love going to the dentist, but she now has an effective coping skill which enables her to stay calm and puts her back in control.

> Mary discovered that imagination, when redirected, can be one of your greatest allies. And once you understand the power of your mind, you can use it to work for you, not against you.

As part of my hypnotherapy training, I watched videos of patients having operations and teeth extractions under hypnosis. No anesthetic – just the power of the mind. Absolutely incredible!

Rest assured that hypno-surgery isn't an area I'm planning to expand into. I'm far too squeamish.

*I fainted when I saw the sheep lungs in my second-year biology class and I think my mum – **Doctor Williams** – was a bit disappointed!*

 ## Krishnan Guru-Murthy: Stepping onto the Dance Floor 

In 2023, news presenter Krishnan surprised many when he agreed to be a contestant on the BBC's *Strictly Come Dancing*.

Even those who knew him well didn't see this coming!

Krishnan has already explained (back in Chapter 10) how he manages the pressure of live TV and reporting from conflict zones, etc. But taking part in *Strictly* was well out of Krishnan's comfort zone!

At the beginning of Strictly it was terrifying because I knew the stakes were very high, and I could look really stupid. But I quickly realised that if I did my best and tried my hardest, then people would judge me on my effort, rather than my ability. So, what was there to be scared of? No one was expecting me to be able to dance perfectly.

Krishnan was understandably nervous in those early weeks. However, fellow contestant **Nigel Harman**, a big fan of mindfulness, had a helpful strategy tucked up his sequined sleeve:

Nigel would take us into the studio and make us focus on what we were doing. He used to say: 'Just close your eyes and think of the dance floor as your friend. Just shut everything else out.'

Nigel helped several of the group with his calming visualisation and positive affirmations: *You know what you're doing. You're really enjoying yourself and you love to dance! You've worked hard this week and have done everything you can. Focus on that.*

Krishnan found Nigel's advice helpful: *I blocked out thoughts about being judged and focused on what I could control. I wasn't asking 'Am I confident I'll do well?' I was asking 'Am I confident that I've done everything I can?*

> **"If something makes me feel uneasy or I've got self-doubt, I want to do it more. There's no better feeling than pulling off something you weren't sure you could do!"**
>
> Angellica Bell

 ### Ricky Wilson: Running for Relaxation 

Ricky maximises his calm moments through movement: *I enjoy running. The regular rhythm of the right–left–right steps helps me with my mental health. I think when I run. I might set off feeling overwhelmed, but by the time I get home, I'm fine!*

TAKE FIVE:

Is there something you do to help you relax? As Ricky proves, it doesn't have to be a sedentary activity. For example, many people find gardening very relaxing – even the repetitive action of weeding can help you decompress. Jigsaws, knitting and colouring are other popular options.

If there is something you enjoy, which also allows you to be fully present and focused, then make time to do more of that activity.

You mind and body will thank you!

 **Katie Thistleton: Bedtime Calm Before the Big Day** 

Katie says her nerves don't appear just before the show, they strike the night before.

I find my anxiety hits me when I'm lying in bed the night before an event. That's when I do guided meditations. I used to think, 'How can this possibly help?' But it does. It stops the panicky breathing that used to keep me awake.

Katie finds calm in perspective too: *I remind myself the audience are human. They'd be scared too if they were doing what I'm doing – and they're on my side.*

That's a timely reminder that relaxation isn't just for showtime, it's for your bedtime too.

***

Q: How can you get better at relaxation?

A: How much time have you got?

Here are two effective, evidence–based self–hypnosis exercises that help your body shift out of fight–or–flight mode and into a state of calm.

Note: If you have a mental health condition, please speak to your doctor before practising self–hypnosis.

Got 10 minutes?

EXERCISE: ONE WORD TO RELAX

You can scan the QR code and I will guide you through this exercise.

Step 1: Set the Scene

Find a quiet space where you won't be interrupted.

Sit or lie comfortably. If seated, have both feet on the floor. Let your hands rest in your lap or by your sides.

Let your eyes gently close when you are ready.

Step 2: Begin with the Breath

◊ Take a slow, deep breath in through your nose… and gently exhale through your mouth.

◊ Allow your breathing to settle into a natural rhythm – slow and even.

◊ With each outbreath, imagine your body softening, releasing, unwinding just a little more.

Step 3: Introduce Your Focus Word

◊ Now, as you exhale, silently repeat the word *'One.'*

◊ Breathe in…

◊ And as you breathe out, gently say the word: *'One…'*

◊ Don't force anything. Just allow the word to float effortlessly on each exhale.

◊ If other thoughts pop in (and they will), simply notice them…and come back to your breath and your word.

Step 4: Continue for 5 – 10 minutes

◊ Inhale....

◊ Exhale...'*One*...'

◊ With each repetition, allow yourself to feel a little more grounded, a little more still.

Step 5: Gently Return

◊ When you are ready, stop repeating the word.

◊ Take a slightly deeper breath in.

◊ Wiggle your fingers and toes.

◊ Exhale with more energy

◊ Slowly open your eyes.

◊ Take a moment to notice how you feel. Appreciate the sense of stillness.

Why This Works

This exercise was devised by Dr Herbert Benson at Harvard University and he proved that repeating a neutral word like 'One' helps quiet the internal chatter and anchors your attention. This exercise gently trains your body and mind to access a state of calm on demand, and with practice, it becomes easier and quicker to reach that state – even in stressful moments.

> *If you are really short of time, even doing this exercise for one minute will still achieve a calming effect.*

Only got 5 minutes?

This body awareness technique activates the natural relaxation response. It is ideal for anxious moments – just before you speak, head into a meeting, or to help you wind down after a long day.

EXERCISE: QUICK CALM – HEAVY AND WARM 

 You can do this exercise sitting or standing. Your eyes can be open or gently closed.

How to Do It

1. Take a breath in through your nose...and exhale slowly through your mouth.

2. As you continue breathing gently, say to yourself (in your mind): *My arms feel heavy...my legs feel heavy.* Pause...let the feeling settle.

3. Now say: *My arms feel warm...my legs feel warm.* Pause again...just notice what you feel.

> 4. Repeat the phrases once more – slowly and softly in your mind: *heavy...warm...calm.*
>
> 5. Take one more deep breath. Then open your eyes and return to your day.

Why It Works

Your body listens to the thoughts you feed it. By imagining sensations of warmth and heaviness, you signal to your nervous system that it is safe to relax. This activates a physiological state that calms your heart rate, relaxes your muscles and settles your mind.

TAKE FIVE:

If you tried both exercises, did you find one of them more effective and relaxing?

Being able to relax your body at will is an incredible and very underrated superpower.

This is another important skill to add to your Confidence Toolkit.

KEY TAKEAWAYS:

◇ It is physically impossible to be anxious and relaxed at the same time.

◇ Beck's theory shows that anxiety increases when you overestimate the threat and underestimate your ability to cope.

◇ The key difference between confident and anxious people is their belief in their ability to cope.

◇ Mindset matters: saying *It'll be alright on the night* sets the stage for calm.

◇ Regular relaxation techniques – like self-hypnosis, movement, or mindfulness – help train your nervous system to respond more calmly.

◇ You don't need to feel confident to begin. You just need to feel calm enough to show up.

Hopefully you are feeling pretty relaxed right now, so why not capture those feelings (and how you achieved them) by making a few notes on the next page or in your journal?

If you could press rewind on a past slip-up and laugh at it like a funny outtake, which moment would you choose?

3

Fear Factor

"Do more of what you fear, and you will fear it less."

Rick Adams

Most people have a fear that even the mere thought of it triggers that unwelcome knot in your stomach, sweaty palms and a racing heart!

For me, it's the idea of being a stand-up comedian.

I know a few comedians and am so impressed by their ability to walk out on stage with the confident expectation that they will make the audience laugh.

I use a lot of humour in my work (as it is a great way to make a human connection) but I could never dream of doing stand-up comedy. The fear of the anticipated embarrassment is a complete deal-breaker for me.

But what is interesting is that the symptoms I just described – the knot in your stomach, sweaty palms and a racing heart – can be interpreted in two very different ways. It all depends on the context.

When I think about doing stand-up comedy, I interpret those symptoms negatively as nerves. But if I were hiding behind a sofa, about to jump out and yell *Surprise!* at a birthday party, those same sensations would feel like excitement.

Same symptoms. Different meanings. It is up to us to decide which one we choose!

Which will you choose?

Fear is Learned

As newborns, we only have two fears: falling and loud noises. These are survival instincts.

Every other fear is learned. Whether that's through our own personal experience, from observing others or from the environments we grow up in.

Of course, some fears are justified. If you live in Australia, being wary of the deadly funnel-web spider is a sensible precaution. However, in the UK, where there is no real reason to fear spiders, arachnophobia is a learned fear and one which many clients bring to hypnotherapy.

> *I enjoy helping clients to overcome fears like arachnophobia. It is incredibly rewarding to help someone remove a barrier that has been holding them back.*

One of the first things to establish is: How valid is this fear?

Often, it can be too triggering to even think about. But, in the safe space of a hypnotherapy session, we can explore where it began and whether it is still valid today.

This process can be revelatory. Sometimes, just seeing that the fear has no factual foundation is enough to reduce its power. This is a significant step towards more positive thoughts, feelings and behaviours.

Client Case Study: Phoebe, Paul and Emma – Facing their fears of being trapped

Cleithrophobia is the intense fear of being locked in or unable to escape and is a common issue I've helped my clients address. Cleithrophobia is different to claustrophobia, which is the fear of confined or small spaces.

Phoebe's story

Phoebe's fear was of trains and trams. Once the doors closed, she feared she had no way out.

Paul's story

Paul's fear centred on flying, but not the flight itself. His fear trigger was the moment the seatbelt sign switched on and he felt trapped in his seat.

Emma's story

Emma dreaded the London Underground, so instead relied on buses, even though it cost her hours of extra travel time every day.

Three different situations but all three shared the same underlying issue: catastrophisation and the fear of losing control. I worked with each of them. We practised mindfulness techniques to anchor them in the present, calming strategies to reduce panic and positive affirmations to reframe their thinking.

Phoebe, Paul and Emma each experienced their own 'light bulb' moment, discovering that their fears existed only in their imagination. And the great thing about proving to yourself that you can overcome one fear is that it creates a ripple of confidence which extends into other areas of your life too.

Confidence nurtures confidence!

TAKE FIVE:

Is there anything which triggers a fearful reaction in you? If so, ask yourself if it is a legitimate fear? What is the likelihood of it ever happening?

Conversely, can you think of an occasion where you overcame your fear? What can you learn from that experience?

Q: What is the difference between a Fear and a Phobia?

A phobia is a more extreme version of a fear. It is excessive, persistent and distressing.

According to the NHS: *A phobia is an overwhelming and debilitating fear of an object, place, situation, feeling or animal. They are more pronounced than fears. They develop when someone has an exaggerated or unrealistic sense of danger.*

In simple terms:

◊ A fear can be intense, but you might still be able to manage it.

◊ A phobia is so strong that it can disrupt your daily life.

The Anxiety Cycle

Some fears, like my dread of a stand-up comedy, don't affect everyday life. It is unlikely I will ever be forced on stage with a microphone to make people laugh!

However, if your fear shows up in everyday situations, it can quickly spiral into a cycle of avoidance and increasing anxiety.

Let's look at a common example. Imagine you work in Accounts, and you have been asked to present a report at the next quarterly management meeting.

You are experienced and capable, but you have a fear of public speaking. Your anxiety kicks in.

So, you make up an excuse and ask a colleague to present instead – Avoidance.

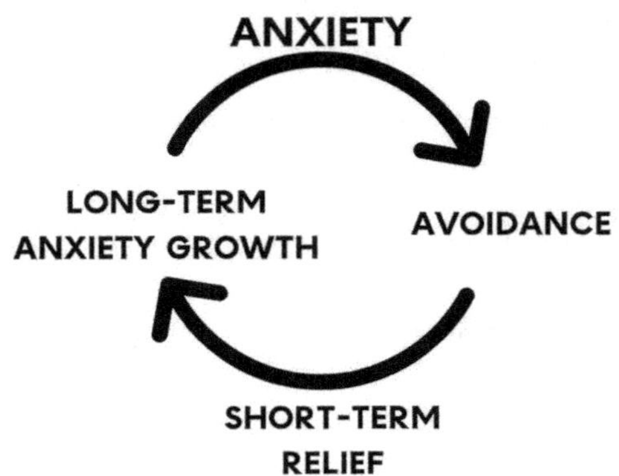

You feel a sense of relief because the pressure is off. But it is short-lived, because that quarterly meeting will come around again in three months' time. And now, having avoided it once, the anxiety feels even worse.

You haven't solved the problem. You have just kicked it away, and (like a snowball) it has grown in size and momentum.

A great way to break out of this cycle is to follow **Susan Jeffers's** advice in her ground-breaking book: ***Feel the Fear and Do It Anyway.***

If you haven't read this book, I highly recommend it. There is also a handy abridged version if you just want the highlights.

Confidence Rule #8:

Fear is a signal, not a stop sign. Notice it, but don't let it decide what you do next.

Client Case Study: Putul – Overcoming the fear of driving

Driving fears are among the most common phobias I see – and they can have a huge impact on everyday life.

Although Putul had been driving for many years, journeys involving motorways, unfamiliar roads or bridges filled her with dread. The thought alone was enough to trigger panic, and she would avoid situations where she was required to drive.

This provided some short-term comfort, but in reality, she had just kicked the can further down the road.

We used hypnotic desensitisation and creative visualisation to rehearse those journeys in her imagination. As you have now learned, the body responds to imagined experiences as if they are real, so her nervous system was able to practise calmness in situations that previously terrified her. By combining this with relaxation techniques and positive affirmations, Putul gained the confidence to drive those routes in real life.

The breakthrough was striking. Once she had proved to herself she could do it, the fear evaporated almost instantly. Because, if you can change the story in your mind, you can change the outcome in real life.

EXERCISE: MOVEMENT-BASED GROUNDING – STEP, SHAKE, BREATHE

When fear starts to rise and your thoughts feel scrambled or your body wants to freeze, this simple movement-based grounding technique can help you reset – fast!

Use it before a big meeting, a performance or anytime fear feels overwhelming.

Step 1: Stand and Shift

◊ Stand with your feet shoulder-width apart.

◊ Slowly shift your weight from one foot to the other – left to right.

◊ Feel the ground beneath each foot. Breathe slowly.

Step 2: Shake it Out

◊ Start by shaking your hands as if flicking off water.

◊ Let the movement travel up to your arms, your shoulders, your neck.

◊ Roll your shoulders. Let tension fall away.

◊ Just 10–15 seconds of loose movement is enough.

Step 3: Breathe and Focus

◊ Take a slow breath in through your nose for a count of four.

◊   Hold for four.

◊   Exhale through your mouth for six.

◊   Drop your shoulders as you breathe out.

◊   Repeat once or twice more.

Optional mantra: Say quietly to yourself: *I am here. I am safe. I can move through this.*

Why it works: This resets your nervous system. Movement breaks the freeze response. Breath calms your heart rate. Your body sends a message to your brain: *I'm in control.*

"Embrace the fear!"

Jez Edwards

 **Celebrity Spotlights:** 

Rav Wilding: From Police Officer to Presenter

With his military and Metropolitan Police background, **Rav Wilding** was the perfect choice of presenter for the live–action CBBC series *Hero Squad*. It was a physically and mentally challenging series where a group of pre-teens trained as first responders with each of the UK's emergency services.

By 2012, when *Hero Squad* started filming, Rav was an established and experienced TV presenter. However, rewind to when his TV career started, on BBC's **Crimewatch** in 2004, and things were very different.

In his interview with **Josh Barry** for ***Beyond the Title***, Rav explained: *I wasn't prepared for the nerves of live TV. It was the scariest thing of my life! My heart was beating so hard you could hear it on my microphone!*

This, from someone who had been in the British Army and was still a serving police officer, indicates just how powerful fear can be!

Michelle Ackerley: Riot-Tested

Michelle also faced fear early in her presenting career when she joined **Crimewatch Roadshow** alongside Rav: *Doing live shows for the first time was petrifying! One day I'd be abseiling down the side of a building and the next, I would be with the RNLI in a capsizing boat.*

But her most terrifying moment came during a live riot training exercise: *I was fully kitted up in riot gear, ready for a live demo involving firebombs. I had done all my preparation and attended all the safety briefings, but I hadn't anticipated the comms going down.*

I couldn't hear Rav or communicate with the gallery. On live TV, one of the bombs came over my shield and landed at my feet. It released a noxious gas and I couldn't speak!

It was chaotic. I couldn't breathe, couldn't see and couldn't talk. I finally managed to say, 'Back to you, Rav' and collapsed into the back of a police van.

Michelle thought she had ruined everything. Then her phone rang. It was the BBC Commissioner: *He said it was the best bit of live TV he'd seen in ages! I had no idea why. But then I realised that no one could tell how frightened I was. The fear was all in my head. It hadn't shown on camera. That was a powerful lesson.*

Lauren Layfield: Living the Nightmare!

I think that the perfect ending to this chapter is this reassuring anecdote from Lauren. Because her experience proves that even if the worst does happen, it is never as bad as you imagined.

*I was booked to present at **BAFTA**. I was waiting, microphone in hand, and got the cue to walk up onto the stage. I made it up about two of those steps: 'HELLO EVERYONE AND WELCO...'. I tripped and hit the deck – hard!*

This was my literal nightmare. But I got up, laughed, made a joke and carried on. And guess what? The world kept turning.

KEY TAKEAWAYS:

◊ All fears (apart from falling and loud noises) are learned. So, all others can be un-learned.

◊ Phobias are more intense, disruptive versions of fear.

◊ Avoidance brings short-term relief but increases long-term anxiety.

◊ Courage isn't the absence of fear. It is feeling the fear and doing it anyway.

◊ Even seasoned professionals get scared, but they still show up.

◊ You can feel fear without showing fear. That is a powerful thing to know

Well done for *feeling the fear and reading this chapter anyway!*

Now take a moment to reflect and jot down any notes. I find that writing thoughts down reduces the power they have over me.

Reflection Question:

What situations trigger the strongest fear response for you, and what small step could you take to face one of them with more confidence?

2

Question Time

The impact a question has on our anxiety levels depends entirely on the context in which it is asked.

Imagine...you are out for drinks with friends, and someone asks, *Do you want ice and lemon in that?* You probably answer without even thinking. It is a low-stakes social interaction with no consequences attached.

Likewise, answers to questions like:

◊   How was your holiday?

◊   Did you see **Coronation Street** last night?

◊   What's the name of your dog?

...tend to roll off the tongue without much effort. You might have dozens, if not hundreds of these back-and-forth conversations every day without a flicker of anxiety.

So, why is it that in some situations, even the *idea* of asking or answering a question can make your heart race and your mouth go dry?

When Questions Feel Threatening

For many people who experience social anxiety, the fear doesn't come from the question itself, it comes from what they believe the question represents. In their minds, being asked something – especially in a public or high-stakes setting – feels like they are being tested or judged.

Social anxiety is driven by the fear of negative evaluation. Research shows that people with social anxiety tend to focus their attention inwards, scrutinising what they are saying, how they are coming across and imagining what others might be thinking of them. This internal focus fuels a cycle of worry and self-doubt.

Do any of these thoughts feel familiar?

◊   What if I say something stupid?

◊   What if they realise I don't know the answer?

◊   What if everyone is looking at me?

When you are stuck in your own head like this, even the most innocent question can feel like a spotlight is being shone directly on your insecurities.

But here is the good news: there is a way out of that cycle and it starts with shifting your focus externally.

> ## Confidence rule #9:
>
> ## Flip the Focus. When you make others feel at ease, you start to feel at ease too.

In Chapter 7 (First Impressions), we explored how your focus of attention impacts how confident you feel. Directing your attention outward is one of the fastest ways to calm your nerves and ground yourself in the moment.

The same applies to questions.

When you are in a conversation or a group setting, try to focus less on how you are coming across and more on the other person's words, tone or body language. Notice their enthusiasm. Listen to their story. Get curious. When your brain is genuinely engaged with what they are saying, your anxious inner voice tends to calm down.

EXERCISE: QUICK CONFIDENCE-BOOSTERS FOR SOCIAL SITUATIONS

If you dread those awkward pauses in everyday conversations, here are a few simple techniques that can help:

◊ **The 3-Second Rule:** Don't overthink it. Respond or ask a question within three seconds before anxiety has time to build.

◊ **Ask First:** If you are nervous, start by asking *them* a question. It takes the pressure off you and gets the conversation flowing.

◊ **Name + Detail Trick:** When someone mentions something, repeat it and ask a follow-up, e.g. *You've got a cavapoochon. What's their name?*

◊ **Keep a Topic Toolkit:** Prepare a couple of neutral topics that you can call on when conversation stalls. Stay away from more divisive subjects, e.g. politics and religion, and stick to safer ground by talking about your family, pets, holidays, hobbies, favourite TV shows, books and occupation. As a last resort, you can always talk about the weather!

Remember, conversation isn't a performance; it is a connection.

TAKE FIVE:

What topics do you find it easy to talk about? Any broad themes or common factors? Having a few *Did you know…?* interesting snippets of information about a couple of neutral topics are always handy to casually drop into conversation.

Why Conversations Matter

Being able to hold a natural conversation isn't just about being friendly, it is a key element of building trust, rapport and confidence.

Whether you are meeting a new colleague, chatting in the queue at Tesco or attending a networking event, being able to exchange a few relaxed sentences can change the energy of an entire interaction.

And here is another confidence secret: conversational skill isn't something you are born with either. It is something you can learn and practise.

 ## Helen Skelton: Finding Common Ground 

When it comes to starting conversations, everyone has something that lights them up – a football team, a hobby, a TV show. Finding that common ground is the best place to start.

I'd always go for easy, open-ended questions like, 'What's your weekend looking like?'

I'm definitely guilty of filling the gaps sometimes, but it's not always necessary. Let people talk – and really listen.

Helen's advice is a great reminder that confidence in conversation isn't about saying more, it is about asking with curiosity and listening with genuine interest.

Active Listening: Your Secret Weapon

One of the most effective ways to improve your confidence in conversations is to become a better listener.

> ## "We have two ears and one mouth so that we can listen twice as much as we speak."
>
> Epiticus

Active listening is about listening to understand, not just waiting for your turn to speak. It is a skill that can completely transform how others see you and how you feel about yourself.

Here's how to practise it:

- ◊ **Make eye contact** (without staring).

- ◊ **Nod or react naturally** to show you're engaged.

- ◊ **Repeat back or paraphrase:** e.g. 'So, you started your own business during lockdown?'

- ◊ **Remember it's a two-way process.** Don't dominate the conversation or bombard the other person with relentless questions.

- ◊ **Ask an open question based** on what they've said: e.g. 'What made you choose that model of washing machine?'

Studies show that when someone feels truly heard, their perception of the listener improves significantly. One study found that active listening increased feelings of empathy and understanding, even when people disagreed. So, if you are ever unsure what to say, remember: being present and curious are more powerful than trying to say the 'perfect' thing.

 ## Angellica Bell: Small talk = Big confidence 

As someone who interviews people for a living, Angellica knows that connection is key. Her top tip? Have an informal chat before the cameras roll, especially if you're meeting someone you admire.

*I remember having to interview **Oprah Winfrey** for **The One Show**. Oprah! A total legend. So, I went into the Green Room beforehand and we just chatted – about shoes! When it was showtime, it was brilliant. She was relaxed, I was relaxed, and we had fun.*

A perfect reminder that confidence grows from connection – not perfection.

The Confidence-Building Power of Asking Questions

There is a myth that confident people always have the answers, but that's not true. However, confident people ask better questions – and they are not afraid to do so.

Whether you are starting a new job, sitting in a meeting or learning a new skill, asking questions is how you grow. It is how you clarify, connect and build trust.

Asking questions shows strength, not weakness

Instead of worrying: *What if I look silly?* try reframing it as *What if this question helps me do a better job?*

Also, you don't really know how the person you are talking to is feeling. So, by asking questions and encouraging the conversation, you might also be helping to put them at ease. Double whammy!

'There's no such thing as a stupid question'

We have all heard people say this, but do you really believe it?

Here is the truth: what feels 'stupid' to you might be exactly what others are wondering about but are too afraid to ask.

You are certainly allowed to ask questions like:

◊ Could you explain that acronym?

◊ Would you mind going over that again?

◊ What does that part mean in practice?

You are not being difficult, you are being diligent. Asking questions builds understanding and understanding builds confidence!

By Royal Appointment – HRH The Princess of Wales

A bit of background information, for context:

During my TV career, I was fortunate to work with The Royal Family on several occasions. The first time was in 1989, when I was a Regional News Researcher in BBC Plymouth. I was tasked with organising the Press coverage of **Her Majesty Queen Elizabeth and HRH Prince Philip**'s visit to the Channel Islands.

> *I was always one of the first people Their Royal Highnesses saw when they arrived on a Channel Island and the last person they saw before they left. Then I would jump on a plane and race The Royal Yacht Britannia to the next location!*

In 2017, I worked with The Royal Household again, this time to produce **Their Royal Highnesses, The Prince and Princess of Wales**'s visit to BBC Children's and the Children's Global Media Summit in Manchester. This was when I first met Prince William and Princess Catherine.

Two years later, I was invited to Kensington Palace to meet with **Princess Catherine** and talk about a feature she was going to film for *Blue Peter*. And just like any other contributor, Princess Catherine had questions. She wanted to know what was going to happen and how she should prepare.

> *Having a cup of tea with the Princess of Wales in Kensington Palace and hearing myself say: 'So Catherine, what are you going to do with your hair?' was a real 'pinch me' career moment!*

But this proves my point. It doesn't matter who you are, one of the best ways to learn is to ask questions.

Never guess. Never assume.

Asking Questions in a Group Setting

Q & A sessions after a talk or presentation can feel daunting, especially if you are already nervous about public speaking. But they are also a great opportunity to be visible, show interest and build confidence.

Here's how to approach it:

1. **Prepare a question in advance** in case the floor opens up.

2. **Use a confidence coping skill:** stand slowly, breathe, smile, and speak clearly.

3. **Frame your question positively:**

    ◊ 'Thank you for your talk. I was curious about...'

    ◊ 'What would you say to someone just starting out in XXX?'

If your voice shakes or your face feels hot, that's OK. You still did it, and every time you do, it *will* get easier.

Job Interviews: The High-Stakes Q&A

Interviews can feel like the ultimate pressure-cooker for question anxiety, but they don't have to be.

I have plenty of experience of sitting on both sides of the table and have interviewed hundreds of applicants during my TV career.

The key is to stop thinking of them as tests and start seeing them as two-way conversations. You are not just there to answer their questions, this is also your opportunity to find out whether this role is the right fit for you.

Tips for handling interview questions confidently:

⋄ **Pause and breathe** before you answer. Resist the urge to start talking straightaway. Instead take a few seconds to check you have understood the question and to formulate your answer. Unfortunately, I have witnessed many interviewees who didn't listen to the question or think before answering and instead answered a question which wasn't asked!

⋄ **Use the STAR technique** to structure your answers (more about that coming up).

- ◊ **Tell a confidence story:** an example of a time you handled something well.

- ◊ **Ask your own questions** at the end. Always have one or two prepared.

The STAR Technique

The STAR method is a simple structure that helps you give clear, confident answers to interview questions, especially those asking for examples of your skills or past experience. Instead of rambling or freezing, STAR keeps you on track:

- ◊ **S – Situation**

  Set the scene. Briefly describe the context or background of the example you are going to share.

- ◊ **T – Task**

  Explain what needed to be done and what your specific responsibility was.

- ◊ **A – Action**

  Describe the steps you took, focusing on what you did (not just the team). This is the heart of your answer.

- ◊ **R – Result**

  Share the outcome. Wherever possible, include something measurable (e.g. saved time, improved sales, solved a problem).

Here is an example of how you use the STAR technique to answer an interview question:

Q: Tell me about a time you had to work under pressure.

A: Situation: *In my previous role, we had a key client project due in half the usual time.*

Task: *I was responsible for coordinating the design team.*

Action: *I set up daily check-ins, divided tasks into smaller chunks, and made sure everyone had what they needed to stay on track.*

Result: *We delivered the project on time, the client was delighted and we secured repeat business.*

Now you know how to structure your answers, let's look at the questions you are most likely to be asked and how to start preparing:

Top 10 Most Common Interview Questions

Question	Preparation Tip
Tell me about yourself	Summarise your background and what excites you about the role.
What are your strengths?	Choose 2-3 with real examples.
What are your weaknesses?	Be honest but show growth.
Why do you want this job?	Link your skills, values and enthusiasm.

Question	Preparation Tip
Where do you see yourself in five years?	Share a vision that shows ambition and flexibility.
Why should we hire you?	Be clear about your unique qualities and successful outcomes.
Tell me about a challenge you overcame	Use the STAR format (What was the Situation, Task, Action, Result?).
Describe a time you worked in a team	Highlight your communication and collaboration skills and how these enhanced the outcome.
How do you handle pressure?	Share real coping strategies (e.g. time-blocking, breathing).
Do you have any questions for us?	Always say 'yes'. Ask about team culture or opportunities to grow.

 ## Jez Edwards: Remembering Names 

Whenever I'm a guest on someone else's show, I try to anticipate what I might be asked, says Jez. I always think of relevant stories and try to remember names and places. It sounds obvious, but how often do we forget names in everyday conversations? If you go into an interview unprepared, that will happen, and it sounds disrespectful and awkward.

Jez's advice to anticipate questions beforehand is sensible. However, you can often go a step further and ask for the questions in advance.

Obviously, you can't do this for a job interview. But if you are part of a discussion panel, a guest on a podcast or being interviewed as an expert for TV or radio, then you can always ask the host, presenter or journalist for an outline of the questions they are planning to ask you.

In most situations, the interviewer won't mind sharing this information with you. In fact, it usually guarantees they get a better response than one you have to think of on the spot.

So, always ask for a heads-up. Even if they say 'No', you are no worse off.

 Katie Thistleton: Surviving the Interview from Hell

Even experienced broadcasters have moments where conversations go off script. Katie recalls one particularly tricky interview with a Hollywood actor who didn't appreciate any of her questions.

It wasn't so bad because I was with two co-hosts and we laughed it off. But I reminded myself that everyone's human. No one has the right to be rude and you don't have to shrink just because they're famous.

Katie's top tip for awkward conversations?

Be yourself and say what's genuinely in your mind. People sense authenticity. I like to skip the small talk and go straight for the real stuff.

Genuine curiosity and self-assurance turn any interview – or everyday chat – into connection.

What to do if you don't know the answer

No one has all the answers. Even the most confident presenters and experts sometimes draw a blank.

If you are asked a question you're not sure about, try saying:

◊   That's a great question. I don't have the answer right now, but I would be happy to follow up.

◊   I would need to check that to be certain. Can I come back to you?

◊   I'm not 100% sure, but here's how I'd approach finding out...

An honest answer, like one of the above, is much better than guessing or making something up!

> Honesty is not weakness.
> It is confidence with integrity.

EXERCISE: IT'S TIME TO PRACTISE THE REFRAME

Think of a question that tends to make you uncomfortable. Maybe it's:

◊ What do you do?

◊ Why did you leave your last job?

◊ What are your rates?

Now, try this:

1. Write down two calm and confident ways to answer it.

2. Then flip it: What's a question you could ask in return?

3. Finally, get used to saying things out loud. Practise having casual conversations in low-risk situations, such as at the school gates at pick-up time or making a coffee in the communal kitchen at work.

> ## Remember:
>
> Confidence isn't about having all the answers. It's about showing up, being curious and knowing that you can handle whatever comes next.

KEY TAKEAWAYS:

◇ **Questions are part of everyday life** – but the context in which they are asked can make them feel anything from 'no problem' to nerve-wracking.

◇ **Social anxiety often stems from a fear of judgement,** making even simple questions feel threatening. Shifting your attention outward, to the person or the moment, can dramatically reduce this pressure.

◇ **Confidence isn't about having all the answers.** It is about staying present, being curious and responding with honesty and calm.

◊ **Active listening is your superpower.** When you listen with real interest, you take the spotlight off yourself and make deeper, more meaningful connections.

◊ **Ask questions** – in meetings, conversations or interviews. This shows strength, not weakness. Remember: clarity builds confidence.

◊ **Whether you're speaking up in a Q&A or sitting in an interview chair**, preparation, calm body language and kindness to yourself are key.

There are only a couple more chapters to go, but the topics we have covered in this chapter can often trip people up! Take a moment to digest what you have learned and process what you have practised.

When you are asked a question, do you usually focus more on having the 'right' answer or on creating a genuine connection? How might shifting that focus change your response? Are you guilty of answering questions before you have thought about what you are going to say?

If your journal is filling up, feel free to make some notes here.

1

This is Your Life

"Be Yourself. Everyone else is already taken."

Oscar Wilde

The phrase 'be your authentic self' gets bandied about a lot. In fact, I know I have used it a few times already in this book! However, to 'be your authentic self' simply means that you are being true to who you really are – living in line with your values and beliefs. In turn, this creates a rock–solid foundation for real confidence.

Yes, we can all learn from others and be inspired by them – but don't try to copy someone else's path. Instead, focus on being the best You!

Confidence Rule #10:

The most powerful version of you is the most authentic one.

Know what fuels you

Start by considering where you get your energy from. Extroverts tend to recharge by being around other people whereas Introverts need time alone to replenish. Neither is better or worse, it's just how your internal battery works.

Ask yourself:

◊ What activities excite or calm me?

◊ What makes me feel grounded or joyful?

Whether it is rock climbing, walking the dog, baking, reading, going to the pub with your mates, crafting, yoga...the options are infinite! Identify the things which help you feel balanced. Then give yourself permission to do those things. Don't shortchange yourself.

Remember:

You can't pour from an empty cup or keep moving with a flat battery.

Who's in your Corner?

As you continue building your confidence, also take a look at your support system.

Motivational speaker **Jim Rohn** famously said: *You are the average of the five people you spend most time with.*

Ask yourself:

◇ Whose energy is influencing me right now?

◇ Am I surrounded by positive people?

◇ Do I have cheerleaders who champion me and offer honest feedback...

◇ ...or am I spending time with glass-half-empty grumblers who leave me feeling drained?

> *My daughter Chelsea gets fed up of hearing me say it...but I'll say it again: 'Friends should be radiators not drains!'*

Moving out of your Comfort Zone is always easier when you have got solid support behind you. Trusted feedback can also be a powerful motivator – it is easier to track your progress when someone you respect says: *Look at how far you've come!*

Your 24/7 Best Friend: Inner Talk

Your inner voice is with you every second of the day. It is your constant companion, so it is worth your while to make friends with it.

Which brings us to one of the simplest and most effective tools I use with clients...

The Power of Positive Affirmations

Positive affirmations are short, powerful statements that can help rewire your thoughts and support healthy behaviour change. I use them all the time with my hypnotherapy clients – not just for confidence, but also for overcoming fears and building new habits.

Here's why they work

Your body responds to your thoughts. So, if you want to change how you feel or act, you need to start at the source and change your *thinking.* And repetition is key.

Think of affirmations as a way of installing new software into your mind. It takes a few runs to get it embedded, but once it's there, it works away in the background.

Examples of Positive Affirmations:

◊   I am confident, calm and capable.

◊   I speak clearly and express myself with ease.

◊   I am learning to handle nerves with grace.

◊   My voice matters.

◊   I can do this.

◊   I am enough.

◊   I don't have to be perfect to be powerful.

Feel free to choose a couple of these that resonate with you or you can write your own. Always use the first person, present tense and use positive language. Avoid words like *not* or *stop*. For example, *I am calm* is stronger than *I am not nervous*.

EXERCISE: AFFIRM AND ACT

◊   **Pick one affirmation** that feels true – or that you *want* to feel true.

◊   **Say it out loud** every day for one week – ideally in front of a mirror. Say it like you mean it.

> ◊ **Write it down** somewhere visible (bathroom mirror, screensaver, notebook).
>
> ◊ **Pair it with action**: each time you say it, do *one small thing* that reinforces it.
>
> **Example:**
>
> **Affirmation:** *I am growing in confidence.*
> **Action:** Join the discussion in a meeting instead of staying quiet.
>
> **Repeat it. Practise it. Believe it.**

Celebrate and Reflect

It is important to always take time to celebrate your wins, no matter how small they seem. Each step forward deserves recognition. And when things don't go to plan? Don't label it as a failure. Instead, call it what it truly is: a learning opportunity.

Growth is rarely a straight line. Confidence, like a muscle, gets stronger the more you use it. Some days will feel easier than others, and that's OK. What matters most is consistency and kindness, because a little self-compassion goes a very long way.

Always be kind to yourself. Treat yourself the same way as you would your best friend.

You've Got This

Change will sometimes feel uncomfortable, even scary. But remember: when you picked up this book, you already had a goal in mind. That intention was the first spark.

By reading this far, you have certainly gathered valuable tools, strategies and new ways of thinking to help strengthen your self-belief. That is a powerful first step. Now your task is to keep the momentum alive.

As you move forward, remind yourself often:

See it. Feel it. Believe it. And then...Go out and do it!

TAKE FIVE: 

At the start of this book, I asked you to gauge where your confidence level was, on a scale from 0 – 10 (0 = Zero confidence, 10 = Maximum confidence)

Before you flick back and check what you wrote, ask yourself: *What level is my confidence at now?*

Now go back to your notes, compare scores and appreciate how far you have come!

KEY TAKEAWAYS:

◊ Authenticity is your foundation. Confidence grows when you stop performing and start aligning with who you really are.

◊ Protect your energy – surround yourself with radiators, not drains.

◊ Your inner voice shapes your reality – make it encouraging, not critical.

◊ Affirmations are powerful tools.

◊ Repetition + Action = Transformation.

◊ Progress is more important than perfection. You are already further along than you were yesterday.

That's it! You now have everything you need to create the life and confidence you want.

So go on, take everything you've learned and be your confident, authentic self – because *This Is Your Life!*

TOMORROW'S WORLD:

In the introduction of this book, I asked you to identify your *Tomorrow's World*. What was your ideal end goal? (If you need to, go back and remind yourself what you said).

Q: Does that goal feel more achievable now?

If you've been making notes as you have moved through the chapters, your progress will be obvious. Feel proud of how far you have come.

Reflection Question:

Take a few more moments to consider your answers to these questions:

◊ *Which tool or technique from this book will you carry forward first? How will you put it into action?*

◊ *If you imagine your future self, looking back a year from now, what would they thank you for starting today?*

0

That's a Wrap!

I often used to feel a bit sad at the end of production on a TV series.* After all the long hours, creative challenges, last-minute fixes and team camaraderie, it was suddenly over. The crew would head off to new shoots, the production team reassigned, the paperwork would be filed and that shared focus to create something brilliant would dissolve.

> *Although – trust me – there were definitely a few shows I couldn't wait to see the back of!*

I feel a little bit like that now because we have come to the end of this book. But this isn't the end of your story, it is the start of your next chapter.

You now have the tools, techniques and insights to build real, lasting confidence. You have learned how to shift your mindset, manage nerves, boost your communication skills and show up as your authentic self.

So now it is time to take what you have learned and put it into practice. Small steps. Consistent effort. And self-compassion.

"Take small steps and you'll get there."

Ade Adepitan

 ## Ade Adepitan MBE: One Shot at a Time 

When I was training for the Paralympics, it was all about trying to accomplish small wins every day. I would go on the basketball court and shoot 400 shots. The next day I would aim for 401.

It's just one shot better, but over time that builds up a portfolio of confidence. You know what you're capable of, because you can look back and say: 'I've done this before. I've achieved it. I've succeeded every day for the last year.'

And as you do that, your confidence builds and builds.

Just one win a day is all it takes.

Learning from others

Some life lessons you have to learn the hard way. It is a process of trial and error and inevitably there are always things you have learned by the end that you wished you had known at the the start!

So what would some of our celebrity contributors liked to have known when they first stepped into their spotlight?

"Some days you'll win and some days you won't win – but always be your own person."

Ted Robbins

"Just focus on the fact that you can do this."

Michelle Ackerley

"Knowledge conquers fear."

Angela Lamont

"Be natural. Be you."

Mark Wright

"Make time for a pre-show nap! It'll calm your nerves."

Les Dennis

"Perhaps you can't do what they do…but no one can you what you do."

Helen Skelton

"We're all human and people are always thinking about themselves more than they are thinking about you."

Katie Thistleton

"It's a role of a lifetime. I love it, but it'll take preparation and practice."

Ricky Wilson

"Confidence is overcoming self-doubt, not pretending it doesn't exist."

Angellica Bell

"There's not much difference between being watched by a handful of people you know and being watched by millions of people you don't know."

Krishnan Guru-Murthy

"Don't take yourself too seriously in this industry, because it'll be over in flash."

Mark Rhodes

"Nerves are just a sign that what you're doing is important to you. Embrace them."

Jez Edwards

"Believe that things will go well. If you keep thinking: 'Don't screw this up. Don't screw this up.' Guess what will happen."

Rick Adams

THE CONFIDENCE CHECKLIST

What you have learned in this book

Here is a handy, at-a-glance recap of everything we have covered. Keep this as a checklist and a reminder of how far you have come.

Mindset Matters

- ◊ Confidence isn't about perfection, it is about belief.
- ◊ Your thoughts create feelings, which shape your behaviour.
- ◊ Reframe negative thoughts into more helpful ones.

Manage the Fear

- ◊ Fear is normal – but it is not a stop sign.
- ◊ Use body-based tools (like breathing and movement) to ground yourself.
- ◊ Visualisation and self-hypnosis can calm your nerves and sharpen your focus.

Master Your Mindset

- ◊ Shift attention *externally* to reduce anxiety.
- ◊ Confidence starts with where you place your focus.

Own Your Voice

- ◊ Speak clearly and with intention.
- ◊ Use vocal warm-ups, pacing and power pauses.
- ◊ Experiment with tone, energy and expression to bring your voice to life.

Face the Spotlight

◊ Use breathing and body language to manage nerves and shine when presenting.

◊ Preparation + Mindset = Poise under pressure.

Rehearse with Intention

◊ Rehearse out loud – not just in your head.

◊ Practise as you want to perform.

◊ Use creative visualisation/mental rehearsal.

Answer with Confidence

◊ Practise how to handle questions, interviews and social situations calmly.

◊ Use active listening and ask questions to stay in control and connected.

Affirm and Act

◊ Use positive affirmations daily to rewire limiting beliefs.

◊ Speak kindly to yourself – your inner voice sets the tone for your outer self.

Be Authentically You

◊ You don't need to be anyone else.

◊ Understand your strengths, manage your energy and surround yourself with radiators, not drains.

If you need a recap of any of these topics, then please go back and review the relevant chapter/s again. This content is to benefit you, so please revisit as often as you need to.

EXERCISE: RE-RECORD YOURSELF ON CAMERA

At the end of Chapter 7 (First Impressions) you recorded a video of you talking to camera for five minutes. You then reviewed and critiqued your performance. Now it is time to repeat the same exercise and see the improvements for yourself.

Here is a reminder of the task:

1. Choose any topic you can talk about for five minutes.

2. Stand or sit up tall and look directly at the camera lens.

3. Take a calming breath, relax and smile.

4. Set a timer for five minutes, press Record and start talking.

5. Remember everything you have learned about body language, pacing, posture, pauses, storytelling, eye contact and volume, and make sure you use your full vocal range.

6. Keep going until the timer ends.

7. Review this recording.

8. Review the original recording and compare both performances.

You can make notes below or in your journal.

Observations from your five-minute video recording:

Did you find it easier/harder this time to talk for 5 minutes? Did what you say make sense?

Consider your body language. Do you look confident? Any distracting mannerisms?

How is your eye contact? Where are you looking?

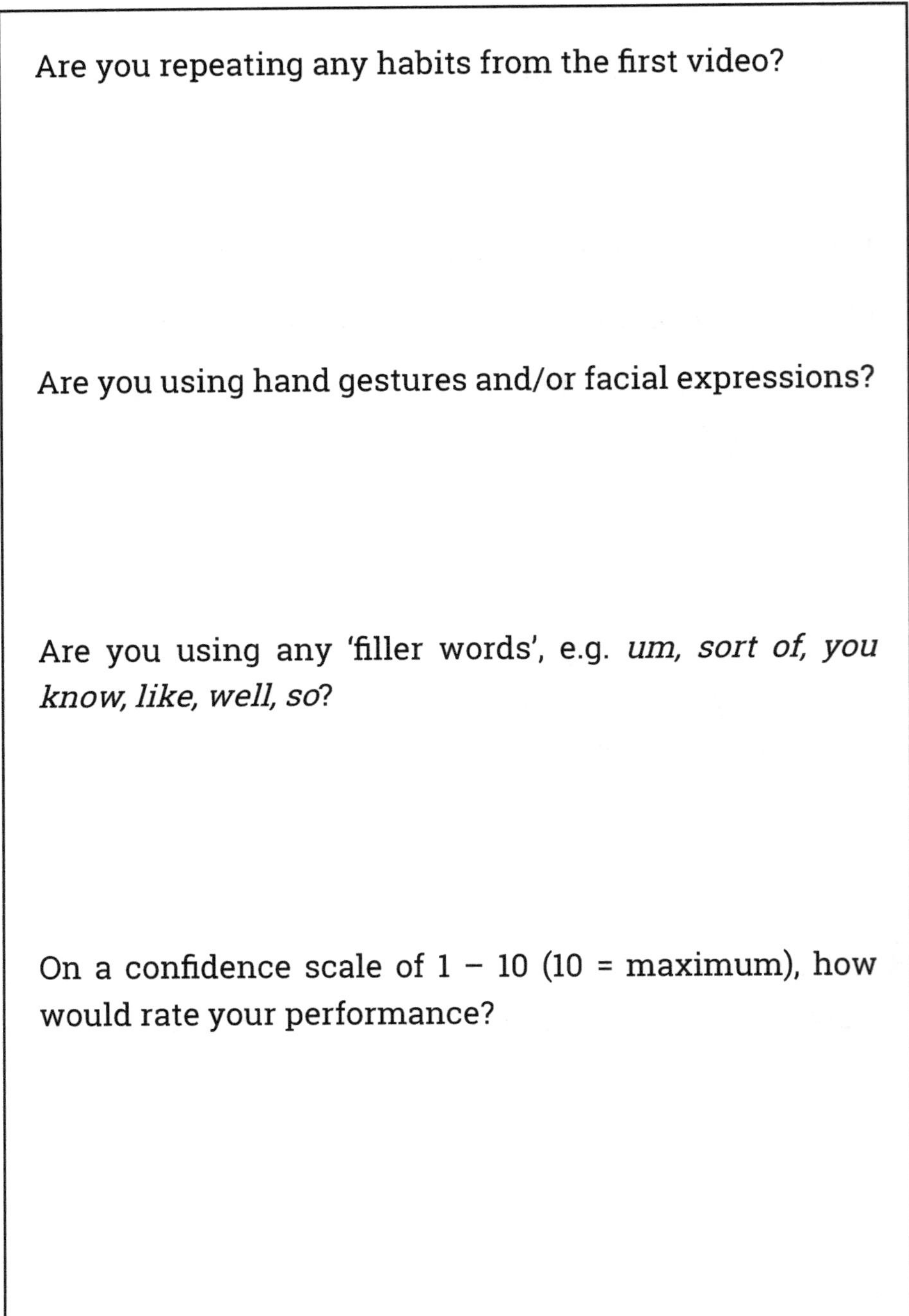

Are you repeating any habits from the first video?

Are you using hand gestures and/or facial expressions?

Are you using any 'filler words', e.g. *um, sort of, you know, like, well, so*?

On a confidence scale of 1 – 10 (10 = maximum), how would rate your performance?

Comparing the two recordings, what improvements do you notice?

What aspects could still do with some improvement?

And Finally:

Congratulations! You took the important first step and picked up this book. You have learned new tools. You have challenged old stories. And you have shown yourself that you are ready to grow.

You have done the hard part.

Now...keep going.

One small win a day is all it takes.

Keep showing up.

Keep speaking up.

Keep believing in yourself, and get ready to…

You're Back in the Room

I would really appreciate getting your feedback about this book and finding out how it has helped you. Please feel free to get in touch and share your individual stories – I would love to read them.

If you would like to connect with me, then here's how:

- ◊ annette@silverbrookhypnotherapy.co.uk
- ◊ https://www.silverbrookhypnotherapy.co.uk
- ◊ https://info.silverbrookhypnotherapy.co.uk/linktree
- ◊ https://www.instagram.com/silverbrook_hypnotherapy
- ◊ https://www.linkedin.com/in/annette-williams-silverbrook
- ◊ https://www.facebook.com/silverbrookhypnotherapy

And, for making it all the way to the end, here is a little something extra. A bonus recording, just for you.

Enjoy it. You've earned it.

Want to Go Further?

If this book has sparked something in you and you are ready to go deeper and continue your confidence journey, then I would love to keep supporting you.

I can offer a range of different services, to suit your needs:

Visit the Silverbrook Hypnotherapy website or contact me directly to find out more about:

◊   1:1 Bespoke Confidence Hypnotherapy

◊   Group Programmes

◊   Overcoming Next-Day Nerves Online Confidence Toolkit

◊   The UnMute Method™ – Stand Up and Speak Out with Confidence

◊   Speaker invitations and workshop opportunities

Whether you are stepping into the spotlight for the first time or rediscovering your voice, I am here to help you!

A final piece of advice:

You have got to know me through the pages of this book, and I hope you now have a better understanding of the cognitive behavioural hypnotherapy approach.

I mention this because I know that for the uninitiated, researching the many different hypnotherapy approaches, can be quite overwhelming.

In the UK, hypnotherapy is a self-regulated field, full of different personalities and bold promises. So, I encourage anyone considering it to do your due diligence. Read reviews, ask for recommendations, and most importantly, find someone you trust and feel safe with.

Thanks and Acknowledgements

I remember my mum saying to me once that *everyone has a book inside them, but most people never get around to writing theirs.* It was just an off-the-cuff comment at the time, but it lodged itself in my brain. And now – many decades later – I have finally written mine. **Thanks Mum and Dad – for *everything*.**

To my wonderful **Family and Friends** – Thank You for your unwavering support, for checking in on my progress and encouraging me to keep going.

Thanks Chelsea – for just being you!

To my 'writing gang' from the Hypnosis Growth Club, who took on the same challenge and kept me accountable. Special thanks to **Sheila Granger** and **Linda Witchell** for your wisdom, encouragement and honest advice.

To **Andrea Haggerwood** for her ongoing professional support.

To my Book Mentor, **Siân-Elin Flint-Freel**, who willingly took on the not-so-small task of giving me feedback and helping me shape this book into what it is now. Without you, I'd still be deciding which font to use!

To **Michelle Catanach** for the cover design and typography.

To the team at **Prism Studios** for producing the videos to accompany this book

To the talented **presenters and performers** who responded so generously to my (many!) emails and messages – Thank You for sharing your stories so openly and helping bring this book to life.

And finally, **Thank You** for choosing this book and trusting me to help you unlock your confidence. I sincerely hope it has sparked something inside you.

Good Luck!

Annette x

About the Author

Annette Williams is The Confidence Hypnotherapist and founder of **Silverbrook Hypnotherapy**.

Before becoming a cognitive behavioural hypnotherapist, Annette had a distinguished thirty-eight-year career in television at the BBC. She spent thirty of those years producing iconic children's programmes like *Blue Peter*, *Going Live!*, *CBeebies Stargazing*, and *The Dengineers*. Her work earned her multiple BAFTA and Royal Television Society awards, a US Emmy nomination, and a treasured Gold *Blue Peter* badge.

Originally from Cardiff, Annette followed her childhood dream of working in children's TV, eventually becoming Head of Factual Formats for BBC Studios – Kids & Family.

In 2023, she left the BBC to pursue her passion for hypnotherapy, retraining with the UK College of Hypnosis and Hypnotherapy. Her unique approach blends creative industry experience with therapeutic techniques to address issues like performance anxiety, public speaking fears, social anxiety and phobias.

As a public speaker, Annette uses her platforms to champion and inspire other professional women to follow their dreams

Annette also teaches at the University of Salford and lives in Cheshire with her daughter, Chelsea, and their dog, Muffin.

(*Silverbrook* was the name of Annette's childhood home in Cardiff. Designed and built by her dad and full of unconditional love and lots of laughter!)

Contributors

Ade Adepitan MBE – TV presenter, Paralympic medallist, journalist, adventurer, author and speaker. For more information: www.johnnoel.com/clients/ade-adepitan

Angela Lamont – Science and Technology TV presenter, Emcee, visibility coach, speaker and live event host. For more information: www.angelalamont.com

Angellica Bell – TV and radio presenter, speaker, podcast host and author. For more information: info@theunderwoods.tv

Helen Skelton – TV and radio presenter, speaker and author. For more information: www.mcsaatchitalent.com/person/ helen-skelton-agent

Jamie Theakston – TV and radio presenter, actor and live events host. For more information: www.jamietheakstonofficial.co.uk

Jez Edwards – Actor, TV presenter, voiceover artist and live event host. For more information: www.jezedwards.com

Katie Thistleton – TV and radio presenter, journalist, author, Mental Health ambassador. For more information: miradorgroup.co.uk/katie-thistleton

Krishnan Guru-Murthy – Journalist, TV presenter, podcast host and speaker. For more information: www.noelgay.com/client/krishnan-guru-murthy

Lauren Layfield – TV and radio presenter, DJ, journalist and author. For more information: www.moneymanagementuk.com/talent/lauren-layfield

Les Dennis – Entertainer, comedian, TV presenter and actor. For more information: www.lesdennis.uk

Mark Rhodes – TV and radio presenter, entertainer, singer and event host. For more information: www.intertalentgroup.com/client/mark-rhodes

Mark Wright – TV & radio presenter, former professional footballer, entrepreneur and speaker. For more information: www.intertalentgroup.com/client/mark-wright

Michelle Ackerley – TV presenter, journalist and event host. For more information: www.insanity.com/collection/entertainment/talent/michelle-ackerley

Ortis Deley – TV and radio presenter, comedian, singer, actor, speaker and event host. For more information: katie.camp@talenteverywhere.com

Rav Wilding – TV presenter and voiceover artist. Former soldier and police officer. For more information: www.talent4media. com/talent/rav-wilding

Rick Adams – TV and radio presenter, performance coach, speaker, creative, illustrator, trainer and event host. For more information: www.rickadamsonline.com

Ricky Wilson – Singer, TV and radio presenter and artist. For more information: www.redlightmanagement.com/artists/ kaiser-chiefs

Sally Gray MBE – TV presenter, events host, media trainer, motivational speaker and podcaster. For more information: www.presentersinc.co.uk/aboutus

Sam Nixon – TV and radio presenter, actor, singer and food influencer. For more information: www.sirentalent.co.uk/ samnixon

Ted Robbins – Actor, comedian, radio broadcaster, speaker, live event host and writer. For more information: www.champions-speakers.co.uk/speaker-agent/ted-robbins

References

Beck, A. T. (1976). *Cognitive therapy and the emotional disorders.* International Universities Press. *Referenced in the discussion of how thoughts influence feelings and behaviours in the 'Master(your)Mind(set)' chapter.*

Clark, D. M., & Wells, A. (1995). **A cognitive model of social phobia. In R. G. Heimberg, M. R. Liebowitz, D. A. Hope & F. R. Schneier (Eds.),** *Social phobia: Diagnosis, assessment, and treatment* (pp. 69–93). Guilford Press. *Cited in the 'Question Time' chapter to explain how social anxiety involves internal focus and fear of negative evaluation.*

Jeffers, S. (1987). *Feel the fear and do it anyway.* Ballantine Books. *Referenced in 'Fear Factor' to encourage readers to reframe fear and take action, reinforcing the principle that confidence grows through action.*

Salter, A. (1949). *Conditioned reflex therapy.* Creative Age Press. *Discussed in 'Faking It' when introducing behavioural confidence strategies and the 'acting as if' principle.*

Benson, H. *The Relaxation Response.* Harvard University. Brigham and Women's Faulkner Hospital – *Benson Relaxation Response exercise as explained in 'It'll Be Alright on the Night'*

Weger, H., Castle Bell, G., Minei, E. M., & Robinson, M. C. (2014). *The relative effectiveness of active listening in initial interactions.* International Journal of Listening

PositivePsychology.com. *Active Listening: The Art of Empathetic Conversation.* (n.d.) Positive Psychology article. Used in the 'Question Time' chapter to support the benefits of active listening in building trust and empathy.

Additional sources:

Begin Again with Davina McCall. *Jamie Theakston: How a Cancer Diagnosis Made Me Live Life to the Fullest.* FlightStory – May 2025

Beyond the Title. *Rav Wilding in Conversation.* Josh Barry. March 2020

Other people to check out/additional reading:

Brene Brown. (2012). *Daring greatly: How the courage to be vulnerable transforms the way we live, love, parent, and lead.* Avery. *A powerful exploration of vulnerability, courage, and connection, referenced as an inspiration for living and leading authentically.* Also, watch any of Brene's TED Talks.

Vinh Giang – *Keynote Speaker, Communication Coach & Magician.* www.vinhgiang.com *Founder of Stage Academy, teaching communication and stage presence through the lens of magic and storytelling.*

Shad Helmstetter. (1986). *What to say when you talk to yourself.* Pocket Books.
A foundational self-help classic on how internal dialogue shapes confidence and outcomes.

Vex King. (2018). *Good vibes, good life: How self-love is the key to unlocking your greatness.* Hay House UK.
An accessible and uplifting book on self-worth, emotional awareness, and living a fulfilled life. Also follow Vex King on Instagram.

Mel Robbins (2017). *The 5 second rule: Transform your life, work, and confidence with everyday courage.* Savio Republic.
Mel Robbins' bestselling book outlines a simple, science-based tool to break hesitation and take action. Also check out:

Mel Robbins *The Mel Robbins Podcast.* www.melrobbins.com/podcast

Dr Julie Smith (2022). *Why has nobody told me this before?* HarperOne.
Dr. Julie Smith, a clinical psychologist, offers digestible strategies for managing anxiety, low mood, and emotional overwhelm. Also follow Dr Julie on Instagram: www.instagram.com/drjulie Regular video content offering mental health tools and relatable advice.

Roger A. Straus (1987). *Strategic self-hypnosis: How to overcome stress, improve performance, and live to your full potential.* Prentice Hall Press.
A practical guide to using self-hypnosis techniques for performance and personal development.